BLESSINGS

FOR
FAMILY AND FRIENDS

JOHN D. GARR, PH.D.

To my loving wife Pat for blessing my life
and faithfully sharing my vision and ministry
these forty years.

Published by Golden Key Press
P. O. Box 421218, Atlanta, GA 30342

Copyright © 2009 by John D. Garr

ISBN 978-0-9794514-3-0
Library of Congress Catalog Card Number:
2001012345

All Scripture verses are quoted from the
Authorized King James Version
unless otherwise noted.

Graphic Design by Elizabeth Nason,
Ambassador Productions, Gainesville, FL

Contents

Acknowledgments

I would like to express my appreciation for the blessing of shared insight that has come to me from friends and colleagues in ministry and in academia. Foremost among these is my friend, Dr. Karl D. Coke, president of Redirection Ministries in Charlotte, N.C., who has shared with me valuable insights into the dynamics of blessing. I am also grateful to Dwight A. Pryor, president of the Center for Judaic-Christian Studies, and Dr. Marvin R. Wilson, Professor of Biblical Studies at Gordon College, for their incisive and inspiring teaching on aspects of this subject. I am likewise deeply indebted to Judy Grehan and Beverly Browning for their careful review of the manuscript and for their thoughtful suggestions for its improvement both in content and style. I am also grateful to Elizabeth Nason for her extraordinary gifts reflected in the graphic design of this volume.

Preface

Huddled in a dimly lit corner of an old subway car, she drifted in and out of conscious thought, oblivious to the fact that her eyes had become glazed over like bottomless pools. She was oblivious to the train wheels struggling against the constraints of steel rails, shrieking as they rounded hairpin turns in the blackness of the tunnel. The incessant clickety-clack, clickety-clack penetrated the night, but for her all the rumble and roar was just background noise that she didn't even hear.

A crack in the door had invited a cold, damp draft to paint her cheeks rosy red and to bestow a generous case of the sniffles to her Kleenex-muffled nose. Just as she drifted off to sleep, suddenly she was jolted by a violent burst of air that rushed from her lungs and exploded into the dank night air: Aaah-choo!

"Bless you!" "Bless you!" "Bless you!" "*Salud!*" "*Gesundheit!*" A chorus of reassuring words rose out of nowhere, echoing through the rocking train. Total strangers, who only moments before seemed not even there, suddenly chimed in, adding their exclamations of concern for a dear soul whose breath had momentarily been stolen away.

In one way or another, this scene is repeated thousands of times every day around the world. Is the exclamation *Bless you!* nothing more than a mere social convention? Is it just a hollow, meaningless custom? Or is there something in the human spirit that is designed by humanity's Creator that compels us to bless others? Is there a biblical basis for our occasional, spontaneous outbursts of concern for our fellow humans and our seemingly irresistible urge to speak words of comfort and encouragement not only to family and friends but also to total strangers?

In the ancient world of the Bible, people routinely blessed one another. They spoke blessings over homes, children, land, labors, travels, and other things and over activities of every sort. Blessings were used for greetings and for goodbyes. They were used to seal covenants and to settle conflicts. In following instructions laid out for them in Scripture, the ancient Hebrews did not allow a single day to go by without speaking words of blessing both to God and upon their families and friends.

Even though blessings were common in Bible times, they were certainly not meaningless. The ancients believed that something really happened when they spoke a blessing. They understood that the God they worshiped was a God of blessing. They were also convinced that the God of blessing had given them the power to bless, and they constantly used this gift that God had given them to bring his blessing into the lives of others.

A Lost Legacy

Both Jesus and the apostles maintained this rich tradition in their lives and in the earliest church. Jesus blessed God, blessed his disciples, and blessed children. In essence, Jesus was one who constantly blessed all people and things around him. The apostles also blessed, and they instructed the early Christians to fulfill their responsibility to bless others (Romans 12:14; 1 Corinthans 4:12).

When Christianity began to distance itself from the Israelite community, however, the biblical practice of blessing in everyday life was soon lost. The Greco-Roman world had virtually no tradition of blessing, leaving benedictions to the temple priests and political leaders. The church, therefore, preferred for new converts from this world to retain their own cultural traditions rather than to adopt radically different emphases from the Jewish culture of Jesus and his apostles.

A focus on the institutional church soon replaced the ancient emphasis on family and community. The daily practice of blessing one another in home, village, and congregation was replaced with formal worship led by an increasingly dominant clergy that came to view itself as the Christian priesthood. The priesthood of all believers was replaced with a professional clergy that arrogated to itself practices that for centuries had been the right of all the people.

Back to the Bible!

Today, because of many generations of neglect, the thought of blessing family, friends, and community hardly enters most Christian minds. There is, however, a rich biblical tradition of blessing that is virtually unknown and unused by the average Christian. Unfortunately, most have been robbed of this important aspect of their heritage. As a result, they are impoverished and underprivileged, not able to access rights granted to them in the New Covenant. Millions of Christians have little or no knowledge of the blessing tradition that was foundational to the lives of the ancient Hebrews and to the faith of Jesus and the apostles. Or they are convinced that blessing is something that only priests and ministers can do, and even then, only on rare occasions and in church ceremonies.

Very often the only time that words of blessing are heard in the Christian community is at the conclusion of a worship service, and even then it is seen more as a signal that the exercise is finished than as a true blessing. The words of a benediction often signal only a yawn, an "amen," and a quick retreat into the secular world. Most worshipers are unaware of the far-reaching consequences of spoken words of blessing. As a result, they have been denied a rich and rewarding part of Christian faith and practice.

If we are to understand and benefit from the divine blessing, we must go back to the Bible, not only in word but also in deed. We must return to the biblical understanding of the blessing itself, of the one who blesses, and of the one who is blessed. We will never experience the fullness and richness of our Christian faith unless we first know the Hebrew Scriptures and the history and culture of the people of the Bible.

As a matter of fact, if we don't restore the Hebrew foundations of our Christian faith, we will continue to be victimized, robbed of the richness of our biblical heritage. We will continue to be deprived of the things God has given us to help us draw nearer to him and to one another. But there is a wealth of biblical wisdom and knowledge that awaits us if we refuse to be victims of the past and fully embrace the Hebraic foundations of our Christian faith.

A Deep Human Longing

In a world filled with curses, everyone needs blessing. Lives pained by brokenness and loneliness desperately long for words of blessing and comfort. This is why over 1,000 books on "blessing" are currently on the market. A large percentage of these books promote pagan rituals that only lead people further from the divine truth about blessing and can even bring curses upon those who dabble in them. Christians, however, must reject these counterfeits and recognize that blessings come only from God and that they must be done God's way.

It is high time that the church reexamined the biblically Hebraic blessing tradition that was repeatedly emphasized throughout the pages of the Bible. It is time to restore this scriptural practice to the prominence that it occupied in the ancient biblical families and communities. For the health and well-being of all believers and of the church in general, it is time that believers in the God of Israel reclaim this teaching and its practical application.

In this book, we will help you to understand how the blessing tradition affected the lives of patriarchs and kings and of prophets and apostles in Bible days. You will learn how believers can still use words of affirmation on a daily basis to bring blessings to themselves and to others. You will be amazed at the number of biblical blessings that you can learn to speak into the lives of family and friends, and even total strangers, for that matter.

Get ready! You're going to be blessed, and in the process, you'll learn to be a blessing by blessing others!

Dr. John D. Garr
Pentecost, 2009

CHAPTER I

The God of Blessing

Many people today think of God as a harsh, bitter old man who lives in a land far, far away, a God who is intent upon judging and punishing human beings. They instinctively know that they have failed to do what is right, and they live in fear that somehow God just can't wait to punish them for all the wrong things they have done. This image has been reinforced by organized Christian religion which has focused on sin and divine judgment.

The true image of the God of Scripture is just the opposite. The Almighty is always portrayed in the Bible as a God of love, a God of mercy and loving kindness, and a God of blessing. King David said, "The Lord is good to all: and his tender mercies are over all his works" (Psalm 145:9). John declared simply that "God is love" (1 John 4:8). As a matter of fact, he even declared that is impossible to know God without understanding and manifesting love.

The apostle Paul captured God's blessing nature in these words: "Blessed be the God and Father of our Lord Jesus Christ, who has blessed us with all spiritual blessing in the heavenly places in Christ" (Ephesians 1:3). It is an undeniable fact that God is intent upon blessing all his children with every blessing.

An Unbroken Record of Blessing

We know that God is a God of blessing today because it has always been a part of his nature to bless. The entire Bible is simply filled with accounts of divine blessings lavished upon those who approached God in faith. Since God never changes (Malachi 3:6) and since Jesus Christ is the same yesterday, and today, and forever (Hebrews 13:8), we know that the God who has blessed his children will always continue to do so.

From the very beginning of time, God's original intention for his entire creation was blessing. He blessed the very first human couple, Adam and Eve, and then he provided a paradise for them that was filled with every blessing they could possibly have imagined. Of all the many blessings that God gave them, perhaps his greatest blessing was to create them in his own image and likeness so they could have relationship with him.

God spoke this blessing to humanity immediately after he had created them: "Let them have dominion over … all the earth" (Genesis 1:26). God's blessing to humankind was that they would lead and maintain the earth in God's glory.

They would rule over the earth in the same way in which God rules over the universe with loving care.

God's blessing continued to be manifest upon Adam and Eve even after they disobeyed him. What appeared to be judgment for their sin was actually an act of God's mercy — a blessing in disguise. They were removed from the Garden of Eden specifically to prevent them from eating of the tree of life and then living forever as sinners with the consequence of being eternally separated from God's presence (Genesis 3:22). It was God's love that even protected humanity in its fallen state until the time would come for redemption and restoration through his Son, Jesus.

Even after mankind fell into sin, God continued to speak the blessing of the same good news (the gospel) that he had first spoken to Adam and Eve: "Let them have dominion …" In succeeding generations the gospel of the kingdom was proclaimed to Abraham (Galatians 3:8), to the Israelites (Hebrews 4:2), to the saints (Daniel 7:18, 27), to the apostles (Luke 22:29-30), and to all believers (Matthew 25:34). God has never given up on humanity, and he never will!

Without exception, God's universal intent for humanity, then, has been to bless us with every blessing. Even the judgment upon the wicked came as a result of their wickedness, not from God's design. It has always been the sins of human beings that have separated them from God (Isaiah 59:2). Humans have withdrawn from their Creator into illusions of sin. God, however, has ever sought for those whom he could bless. If God is fixated on anything, it is blessings, not curses. The God of the Bible is the God of blessing.

THE BREATH OF THE ALMIGHTY

When God breathed into Adam's nostrils the breath of life, something amazing happened. More than oxygen filled Adam's lungs. Paul tells us that all Scripture is God-breathed (2 Timothy 3:16). When God's breath brought Adam to life, he also received a deposit of God's Word into the very essence of his being. As a result, the living words of God were in a measure written on humanity's heart from the beginning.

In order to make humanity in his image, God blessed Adam and Eve with the power of reason and placed in them a conscience as a spark of the divine that has since always drawn humanity to God. Even the descendants of Adam who had no direct covenant with God had God's Word in their hearts.

Listen to how Paul described God's amazing original blessing for humankind: "For when Gentiles who do not have the Law do instinctively the things of the Law, these, not having the Law, are a law to themselves, in that they show the work of the Law written in their hearts, their conscience bearing witness and their thoughts alternately accusing or else defending them" (Romans 2:14-15, NAS).

God placed his Word—the very essence of what is "God-breathed"—in Adam and in every subsequent human being. Since the beginning, God's instructions (often called "the law") have been written on human hearts so that their consciences could either condemn or excuse them before God. In the words of Elihu, the breath of the Almighty gives man's spirit understanding (Job 32:8). This insight is the blessing that separates humanity from the animal world.

The Word of God that is implanted in the human heart generates faith for salvation and return to God. Faith comes by hearing God's Word (Romans 10:17). Because God's Word is written on man's heart, it is with the heart that we believe unto salvation (Romans 10:10). Creating faith is entirely God's activity. He alone speaks his Word to us and draws us to himself.

GOD'S IMPRINT ON THE HUMAN HEART

Blessing, then, is implanted into the very fiber of human life. God's likeness and image are stamped in the heart of every human being. His Word constantly speaks blessing into every life and warns against the curse of sin. Both the righteous and the unrighteous of the earth are objects of God's blessings, for he causes the sun to shine on the evil and the good, and he sends the rain upon both the just and the unjust (Matthew 5:45). All human beings are the same; all are equal before their Maker. The only difference in the righteous is that they are saved from sin by God's grace.

This biblical truth is confirmed by medical science. When an echocardiogram of the human heart is made, a startling image is revealed. The tissues that separate the chambers of the heart are aligned in such a way as to form the Hebrew letter *shin* (ש). Among the ancient people of the Bible and their descendants, the letter *shin* has been universally recognized as a symbol for God, for it is the first letter of

GOD'S NAME ON THE HUMAN HEART

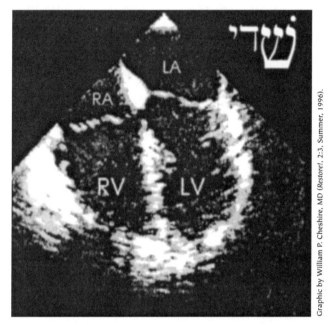

Graphic by William P. Cheshire, MD (*Restore!*, 2:3, Summer, 1996).

In the echocardiogram above, the Hebrew letter *shin* is clearly seen in the tissues that surround the chambers of the human heart. The letter *shin* is the universally recognized symbol for the divine name *Shaddai* ("The Almighty God"), which is seen at top right above.

Shaddai (El Shaddai — the Almighty), one of the most ancient and significant names for God in the Bible.

Is this image a mere coincidence? Or is it evidence that God has left the imprint of his name on the very heart of every human being who has ever lived on this earth? Do all of the more than six billion people living on this planet today bear the image of the God of the Bible written on their hearts? Is there a spark of the divine in all humans that ever draws them toward God and to what they intuitively know is right and good? Does this imprint of the divine on the human heart give an innate inclination toward doing good even in the face of surrounding evil? Is there a blessing inclination in every human heart?

Though the heart of man is so deceitful and desperately wicked that only God can know it (Jeremiah 17:9), still the God of blessing has maintained a spark in men's hearts that becomes a torch of enlightenment through the word of faith (Proverbs 20:27). The human heart is one of the places where God has chosen to place his name, the signature that proves his ownership of all humanity. "The earth is the Lord's and all that it holds, the world and its inhabitants" (Psalm 24:1, TNK). And, all that God possesses is the object of his lavish love poured out in blessing after blessing.

ORIGINAL BLESSING

Despite God's eternal commitment to bless humankind, Adam and Eve's fall into sin has been viewed by most Christian teachers as the defining moment in the history of the human race. And, indeed, the Bible makes it clear that all men are slaves to sin (Romans 3:23; 5:12). King David lamented the human condition that had produced his unspeakable sins of murder and adultery: "I was born with iniquity; with sin my mother conceived me" (Psalm 51:5). The Apostle Paul shared the pain of sin's addiction: "The good that I will to do I do not do: but the evil that I will not to do, that I practice"

(Romans 7:19). The record of human history is clear: "There is none righteous, no, not one" (Romans 3:10).

Since God is the God of blessing, however, he was not content to leave man in his fallen state. While men have almost always been fixated on sin, God has always been focused on blessing. His faithfulness to bless humankind was not blocked by sin. He simply further extended his tender mercy in terms that have never been nor can ever be fully understood. "For God so loved the world that he gave his only begotten Son, that whoever believes in him should not perish but have everlasting life" (John 3:16).

God refused to dwell on the "original sin." He was determined to focus instead on "original blessing." To ensure the fulfillment of his original blessing to humanity, God was manifest in the flesh (John 1:14). In the person of his Son, he overcame sin (Romans 8:3) and offered himself as an atonement for the sins of humanity (Ephesians 1:7). Now, all who come to faith in Jesus are delivered from the power of sin and its curse, and they enter fully into the heavenly Father's blessing.

Humanity's liberation from sin, however, is nothing more than the completion of God's never-ending commitment to bless humanity. From the very beginning, his eternal plan provided for redemption through the sacrificed Lamb of God who takes away the sin of the world (John 1:29). Indeed, Jesus is the lamb slain from the foundation of the world (Revelation 13:8). Before all creation, God had already planned redemption. Adam's fall was foreseen, and provision was made before the fall to fulfill the covenant and blessing.

The life, death, and resurrection of Jesus merely provided the means by which the covenant and blessing that was originally intended could be fully restored to humankind. God, therefore, has never been obsessed with man's sin: he has always been committed to man's blessing.

God is the God of blessing. He always has been, and he always will be. He will never change: he will never compromise his covenant faithfulness that is ever manifest in the blessings he brings to his children. He will never stop blessing his children!

Chapter 2

God's Personal Blessing

The most beautiful blessing in the Bible is the one that God himself composed and dictated to Moses over three thousand years ago. This blessing says, "The Lord bless you and keep you. The Lord cause his face to shine upon you and be gracious unto you. The Lord turn his face toward you and give you peace" (Numbers 6:24-26).

This ancient blessing is so powerful that it has been known among biblical peoples as "The Blessing." What makes it so amazing is not that God spoke it once in history but that God established a system to ensure that it would be pronounced upon all of his children forever. "The Blessing" has been called the Aaronic Benediction because God made Aaron, the high priest, and his descendants, directly responsible for speaking this blessing over the Israelites throughout all their generations.

When the temple was destroyed and the priesthood was dispersed nearly two thousand years ago, responsibility for speaking God's personal blessing upon the children transferred to the heads of families in Israel, while the descendants of the priests continued to make the blessing in corporate meetings. Jewish people have considered each home to be a temple in miniature (*mikdash me'at*); therefore, for centuries they have faithfully spoken God's blessing over their children in their small family sanctuaries, their homes.

THREE BLESSINGS IN ONE

"The Blessing" is really three blessings in one, three separate complete sentences. Since there are three persons in God—Father, Son, and Holy Spirit—it is only fitting that there are three blessings in God's one personal blessing.

The first blessing says, "The Lord bless you and keep you." These words are from God the Father, and they reveal two things about his nature as Father: he is determined to bless and to keep his children. God the Father is the Shepherd of Israel (Psalm 80:1) who guards all of his children and blesses them with unlimited blessings.

The second blessing says, "The Lord cause his face to shine upon you and be gracious unto you." These words of benediction come from the Son of God, the person who put a face on the Father so that when one sees Jesus, he sees the Father (John 14:9). Since "no man has seen God at any time," the "only begotten Son has revealed him" (John 1:18). The Son of God is "the radiance of God's glory and the exact representation of his being" (Hebrews 1:3), for God caused his glory to "shine in the face of Jesus Christ" (2 Corinthians 4:6). It is Jesus who causes God's face to shine upon humanity, and it is uniquely he who brings God's grace into human

God's Personal Blessing

The Lord bless you and keep you.
The Lord cause his face to shine upon you
and be gracious unto you.
The Lord turn his face toward you and give you peace.

יְבָרֶכְךָ ה' וְיִשְׁמְרֶךָ

יָאֵר ה' פָּנָיו אֵלֶיךָ וִיחֻנֶּךָ

יִשָּׂא ה' פָּנָיו אֵלֶיךָ וְיָשֵׂם לְךָ שָׁלוֹם

lives, for "grace and truth came through Jesus Christ" (John 1:17). God the Son causes God's face and his grace to shine upon believers so that they can know and understand God.

The third blessing says, "The Lord turn his face toward you and give you peace." These words are from the Holy Spirit, the person of God who not only reveals but also turns God's face toward humanity and enables humans not only to understand but also to experience God. The Holy Spirit is the agent of God's peace, the peace that passes understanding (Philippians 4:7).

Placing the Divine Name

When God dictated his personal blessing to Moses, he concluded by saying that when the blessing was spoken over the children of Israel, God's own personal name would be placed upon them and he would bless them. While there are many names that men have used to describe God, there is only one name that God chose for himself, the name YHWH (Yahweh). God's personal name means "I am that I am" or "I will be what I will be," or simply, "I will be there."

When "The Blessing" is spoken, God's name (which is no longer spoken aloud but is represented by "The LORD" in Scripture) is repeated three times, once in each of the three blessings in "The Blessing." The thrice-repeated name of God actually places God's name on the one who is blessed, thereby fulfilling God's statement, "They will put my name upon the children of Israel." In ancient times, the priests took God's statement literally. They actually used their fingers to trace God's Hebrew name either on the forehead or in the right hand of the one who was being blessed!

The Name of God

If you choose, you can imitate the priests in the ancient temple by tracing these letters with the index finger of your right hand on the forehead or on the palm of the right hand of the person over whom you have spoken "The Blessing."

What a powerful image! What believer would not want God's name to be written in their foreheads? Indeed, the very last book of the New Testament speaks of those who have "the Father's name written in their foreheads" (Revelation 14:1). Is it possible that by speaking the words of God's Blessing upon our children or over our congregations, we can actually place God's name on them? From this simple text, it certainly appears so!

RESTORING OUR HEBREW LEGACY

"The Blessing" has no magical powers. After all, it was God, not the priests, who blessed. At the end of his instructions regarding the blessing, God said, "*I* [not you] will bless them." The Jewish people of history have always understood that only God can bless. Men can only serve as instruments through whom God can bless.

The divine blessing, however, is not just a mere ceremonial formality. And God did not make it optional. God commanded that his children be blessed throughout all their generations with the specific words of benediction that he formulated and dictated to Moses. This threefold blessing is powerful and eternal. It is the generationally enduring promise of divine favor and all that it provides. It is the very personal blessing from the exalted Sovereign of the universe to even the seemingly most insignificant of human beings.

Why would this blessing be so neglected among Christians when it has always been so important among the Jews? Perhaps in their rush to separate themselves from the

Jewish community, Christians left behind a great part of the Hebrew legacy that was foundational to the faith of Jesus and the apostles. Unfortunately, "The Blessing" is now used almost exclusively as a benediction at the end of a worship service! Even then it lacks the individual personalization of the ancient practice.

There are many wonderful and beautiful benedictions in the Holy Scriptures, including the New Testament. These can and should be repeated over congregations and individuals by those whom God has ordained as leaders in the community of faith. This should not, however, be done to the neglect of the one Blessing that God himself composed and commanded to be spoken upon all of his children forever.

The first place where this Hebrew legacy should be recovered is in the Christian home. Christian parents should imitate their Jewish counterparts by blessing their own children with God's blessing. Secondly, when Christians assemble for corporate worship, leaders should remember God's commandment and speak his words of blessing over them collectively. Even in Christian schools, it is appropriate for teachers to pronounce this blessing on their students just as in ancient times Jewish teachers spoke the blessing upon their students.

When blessings are spoken in obedience to God's instructions, God makes this absolute promise: "I *will* bless them." Is there any doubt that God's Word works? When we do what he says, we reap the benefits. In this case, Christians can enjoy more blessed and fruitful lives if they simply give and receive God's blessing in both home and congregation.

CHAPTER 3

Blessing and Being Blessed

God's blessing nature was clearly manifest four thousand years ago in the life of one man. Abraham was chosen by God and became the first Hebrew when in faith he obeyed God and crossed over the Euphrates and entered the Promised Land. (The word *Hebrew* is from *eber* which means "cross over" or "from the other side.") Abraham was the object of God's covenant and blessing, and he became the channel through whom God would bless "all the families of the earth" (Genesis 12:3). Paul even described Abraham as "the father of us all," both Jews and Gentiles who are believers in the God of the Bible (Romans 4:16).

In Abraham, God established this eternal blessing principle: God lavishes his blessings on his children so that they, in turn, can bless others. Listen to God's promise to Abraham: "I will bless you and make your name great, and you will be a blessing" (Genesis 12:2). God was so intent upon blessing Abraham that he swore an oath by his own name, saying, "Surely blessing I will bless you" (Hebrews 6:13-14). Then he said, "In you shall all the families of the earth be blessed" (Genesis 12:3).

God manifest his covenant and blessing first to Abraham and then through him to the entire world. Abraham was a man of pure faith and faithfulness. He believed God (Galatians 3:6). As a result, God made an everlasting covenant with him. God's blessing was the product of his covenant. Both the covenant and the blessing of Abraham were extended to the entire world through Jesus: "He redeemed us in order that the blessing given to Abraham might come to the Gentiles through Christ Jesus, so that by faith we might receive the promise of the Spirit" (Galatians 3:14, NIV).

Abraham was not blessed by God just for his own personal benefit. God's blessing was given first to Abraham, then to his children, and finally to all the nations of the world. God's immediate intention was to bless Abraham, but his ultimate objective was to bless all those who would imitate the life of faith that Abraham lived.

God's blessing for Abraham became a dynamic model to the nations. God used the one whom he had blessed to become a channel of blessing for all men. His blessing for the Abrahamic family was not solely for their benefit. It was not a scheme to develop a super race to dominate the world. God's covenant with Abraham and his descendants was for the purpose of serving the world with enlightenment and blessing. Abraham's blessing was a blessing to bless.

God's concern for blessing has always been the same, from the beginning to the end. He blessed humanity from the moment of creation, he continues to bless humanity now, and his final act for humanity will be blessing. And he has always blessed the ones he has chosen so that they could bless all of his children.

CHILDREN OF ABRAHAM

Those who have come to faith in Jesus as Lord and Savior have become Abraham's children. "If you belong to Christ, then you are Abraham's descendants, heirs according to promise" (Galatians 3:29) God's promises and blessings for Abraham were not just for his physical descendants; they were also intended for his spiritual descendants. Just like Father Abraham, then, Christians are blessed of God in order to bless others.

Jesus declared that those who are the children of Abraham will do the works of Abraham (John 8:39). If Abraham is our father, then we will manifest the life of faith that Abraham pioneered. When we do, we will find ourselves being the object of God's blessing. Then, we will become channels of God's blessing to others. We will even become God's blessing-bearers to the nations.

Because Abraham had been appointed by God to be a blessing to all the families of the earth, he often found himself engaged in prophetic intercession, imploring God's blessing in the lives of others. This he did for Lot (Genesis 13:8), for Ishmael (Genesis 17:18), and even for Sodom and Gomorrah (Genesis 18:22-33).

Christians today who are of Abrahamic faith will be more concerned about God's blessings to others than they are about themselves. They will be active intercessors, praying that God's blessings will come to all the people of the earth. They will begin by blessing their own families, then by blessing their neighbors and friends, then by blessing their communities and nations, and finally by blessing the entire world!

The Christian's blessing will not even be limited to family, friends, and loved ones. It will even be extended to enemies. Just as Abraham sought God's blessing on Sodom, so Christians should obey the command of Jesus: "Love your enemies, bless those who curse you, do good to those who hate you, and pray for those who spitefully use you and persecute you" (Matthew 5:44, NKJV).

Blessing and Grace

God is the source of all blessing. The means by which blessing is conveyed is divine grace. Nothing that men can do will ever merit God's favor. Grace and the blessing it brings are the outpourings of God's love. God's determination to love and bless is unrelenting and will never be abandoned, nor can it ever be suppressed.

In the New Testament, the Greek word for grace is *charis*, which corresponds to the word *chen* in Hebrew, meaning "favor, grace, charm, elegance, or acceptance." Grace is also implied in the Hebrew word *chesed*, which means "tender mercy or loving kindness." Grace, then, is the focus of blessing. "Grace be unto you," was a common greeting, as well as a benediction from the apostles (Romans 1:7; 16:24).

Man's very salvation is based upon God's grace: "For by grace are you saved through faith" (Ephesians 2:8). This grace is superabundant: "Where sin does abound, grace does much more abound" (Romans 5:20). When sin entered in, God's grace and its resultant blessing were not diminished. If anything, God expanded the range of his grace to account for man's disobedience and to provide a means of ensuring his blessing to all.

The Circle of Blessing

The model of blessing that God first applied to Abraham is clearly demonstrated in the New Testament. God blessed Abraham so he could be a blessing. Likewise, God still blesses all believers so they can bless others, who, in turn, can bless God with thanksgiving and praise.

Blessing is given by God directly to men in the form of his grace (*charis* in Greek). Then, the grace and blessing are transferred to others through the spiritual gifts (*charismata* in Greek) that God has given to humanity. One can even see the word *grace* (**charis**) in the word *gifts* (**charis-mata**) that are described in Romans 12 and 1 Corinthians 12.

The gift of grace blesses the one who receives it, and it empowers him to bless others. Paul observes that all believers have gifts that differ "according to the grace [*charis*]" that is given to them (Romans 12:6). Just like Father Abraham, Christians extend God's grace laterally into the lives of others by being instruments of blessing.

God's blessing, then, is given so that the person who is divinely blessed may, in turn, be a blessing to someone else. In order to bless others, one must become a channel through whom God's blessing can flow. The grace that is delivered vertically from God is then channeled horizontally into the lives of others.

Recognizing God as the only source of all blessing promotes humility and the understanding that we cannot control the capacity to bless. At the same time, it also enables us to become highly available as channels of divine blessing. Those Christians who are the children of Abraham through faith are blessed of God in order to be God's blessing-bearers to others.

The beauty of this experience is that the grace and blessing that are manifest through spiritual gifts never end with either the one who is bestowing the blessing or with the one who is receiving the blessing. Through thanksgiving (*eucharistia* in Greek), the grace and blessing are returned to God who gave them. Observe the word *grace* (**charis**) in word *thanksgiving* (*eu-charis-tia*). Those who are blessed either directly by God or indirectly through chosen and blessed vessels give praise to God. By giving thanks to him, the grace and blessing come full circle. The blessing that came from God returns to God as praise.

This is why Paul said, "In everything give thanks [*eucharistia*], for this is the will of God in Christ Jesus concerning you" (1 Thessalonians 5:18). It is why David said, "I will bless the Lord at all times; his praise shall continually be in my mouth" (Psalm 34:1). The ancient Hebrew people

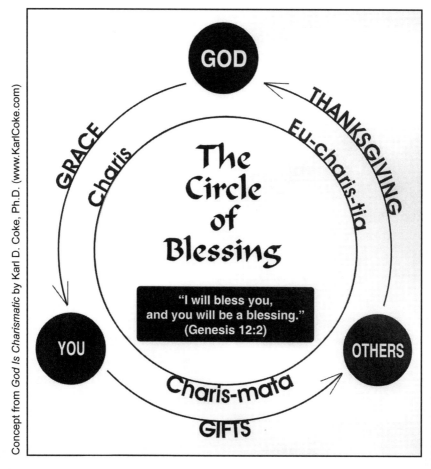

The blessing of God's grace (*charis*) that is given to you is conveyed laterally to others by God's gifts (*charis*-mata) in your life. Both you and they then return the blessing to God in the form of thanksgiving (eu-*charis*-tia), completing the Circle of Blessing.

understood that God was the source of all blessing. That is why they always blessed or sacrificed to him with the voice of thanksgiving (Psalm 26:7; Jonah 2:9).

As we have seen, grace (*charis*) from God is transferred laterally to others through spiritual gifts (*charismata*) so that both the one who is blessing and the one who is being blessed can return the grace to God through thanksgiving (*eucharistia*).

BLESSING RECIPROCITY

It is impossible for a believer to bless someone else without being blessed in return. The divine energy of blessing is reflected from the one who is blessed to the one who blesses. In like manner, blessings can have continuing impact on many others over long periods of time. A blessing for one can even transcend time and become a generational blessing.

God's blessing can never be bottled up. The word of benediction is so powerful that it produces a chain reaction of blessing. This is a part of the divine law of reciprocity: you receive what you give and in the same proportion in which you give. It is impossible to bless without being blessed.

God's blessing is imparted to those who open their hearts to his grace. In turn, these humble souls who have qualified themselves as instruments of God's grace become channels through whom the grace of blessing flows to others. Like Father Abraham, we do not consume the grace upon ourselves. We always release it both to men and to God. We are blessed of God with a view toward blessing others. God expects it, and so do we. We learn to love as Christ did in self-sacrificing service that goes beyond human reason. In blessing others, we are blessed.

Seven Reasons
Why You Should Bless

1) You fulfill the instructions in the Word of God for blessing.

2) You establish and promote a culture and lifestyle of blessing.

3) You maintain a positive, "Good News" mindset by blessing.

4) You manifest the gifts of the Holy Spirit through blessing.

5) You confirm your dependence on God as your source.

6) You reinforce to yourself and to others that God's Word works.

7) You are always blessed even more when you bless others.

CHAPTER 4

Family Blessings

The first place where God's blessings should be pronounced is in the home. For thousands of years this has been the case in Hebrew and Jewish homes. God's first promise to Abraham was this: "In you all the families of the earth shall be blessed" (Genesis 12:3). The Jewish people and their faith have survived centuries of unrelenting persecution solely because of the importance attached to the home as the center for spiritual, social, and intellectual development. The Jewish temple was destroyed, and countless synagogues have been burned. Still, the Jewish home has remained the bedrock of the social and spiritual community.

The Hebrew people highly valued their families and maintained respect for parents, spouses, and children. The family was the unit for nurturing and strengthening individuals. Both husbands and wives profited from the balance of their covenant relationship. Children were nurtured in the security of a stable, loving, and blessed environment.

Christianity, on the other hand, has focused so much of its social and spiritual life on its corporate worship experience that, by default, it has often neglected the importance of worship and other spiritual exercises in the home. This is particularly true of blessing. If words of blessing or benediction are given in Christian circles, they are generally reserved to the clergy. Most Christian parents have just never stopped to think how important their homes are as places for fellowship, study of God's Word, worship, and blessing. Blessing was first a family affair, and it still is!

BLESSING BY FAITH

When Christians think of faith, they envision moving mountains, or they remember the astonishing miracles that are recorded in the Bible. "Now faith is the substance of things hoped for, the evidence of things not seen," they recall from Hebrews 11:1, and they are uplifted by accounts of saints translated, floods escaped, seas parted, and walls flattened. The Bible's "Faith Chapter" speaks of all of these miracles and more that were accomplished by faith.

Right in the middle of all these accounts of astounding miracles, however, are two stories that somehow don't measure up to our images of biblical faith: "By faith Isaac blessed Jacob and Esau in regard to their future. By faith Jacob, when he was dying, blessed each of Joseph's sons, and worshiped as he leaned on the top of his staff" (Hebrews

---

HANDS OF BLESSING

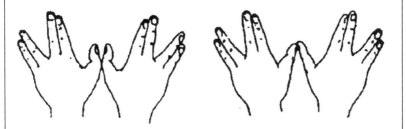

The graphic above demonstrates two ways in which the priests held their hands as they lifted them up while blessing the people with the "Priestly Blessing."

11:20-21, NIV). Could blessing children in the home be an exercise of faith that is on a par with stopping the mouth of lions? Did Jesus perform as great a miracle when "he took the children in his arms, put his hands on them, and blessed them" (Mark 10:16, NIV) as when he said to the raging sea, "Peace, be still" (Mark 4:39)?

HANDS OF BLESSING

It is no coincidence that Jesus "put his hands" on the children when he blessed them. In our modern world, putting one's hands on a child's head or laying one's hands on a friend may seem quaint or outdated, but in Bible days, it was the norm.

The Hebrew people believed that something actually happened when they laid their hands on their children. And their children believed it too! All we have to do is to remember the length to which Jacob and his mother went to have Isaac's hands of blessing laid on Jacob's head (Genesis 27). It is for this reason that Jewish children to this day are taught from a tender age to approach their fathers "with their heads inclined toward their father" to receive God's blessing.

Is there magic in placing one's hands on someone? No, but something does happen. In other examples of the Hebraic practice of "laying on of hands," authority, anointing, healing, and blessing were transferred. Joshua received an element of Moses' authority when the prophet laid his hands on him (Numbers 27:18-23). Timothy received a spiritual gift when the elders of the community laid their hands on him (1 Timothy 4:14).

THE CREATIVE WORDS OF BLESSING

Words have amazing power! They create, either for good or for evil. Negative statements foster negativity and produce undesirable results. Reinforcement from positive words generates optimism and promotes beneficial outcomes.

This is all the more true of the Word of God. It is alive and powerful (Hebrews 4:12). It is creative, the means by which everything that exists came into being (Hebrews 11:3). The Word also sustains all creation (Hebrews 1:3). Once again, God's Word works!

The words of blessing, then, are powerful, especially when they are the words spoken by God himself. When we speak God's words over our spouses, over our children, or over our friends, something dynamic happens. The impartation of blessing creates an environment of positive expectation and produces positive results. God simply honors his Word.

Blessing after Blessing

In the Bible you will find numerous blessings for God (words of praise and thanksgiving). In Jewish tradition, there are over one hundred blessings that can be spoken in praise of God each day. In the Bible you will also find blessings for husbands, for wives, for sons, for daughters, for friends, and for strangers. You will find blessings for special occasions: for family meals, for holidays, for births, for weddings, for rites of passage, for graduations, for bereavement. There is a blessing for virtually everything.

How do you do it? It's really simple. Here's how: Take someone's hand or lay your hand on them respectfully. Look into their eyes. Then speak the words of biblical blessings, or create your own blessing from your heart. Don't worry about how "professional" you may or may not sound. Your heart should be talking, not your brain! Affirm the good that you recognize in the person you bless, and speak the hope of your heart for them. As a child of God, you are authorized to speak these words of Scripture: "The blessing of the Lord be upon you; we bless you in the name of the Lord" (Psalm 129:8).

There's nothing stopping you. Just do it.

A Sanctuary of Blessing

The home is not merely a social convention: it is a holy place, a sanctuary of blessing. As in Jewish tradition, every Christian home already contains an altar. It's the table where the family gathers to eat food. God's altar was called a table by Malachi (1:7,12) and by Paul (1 Corinthians 10:21). If God's altar is a table, then the family table can also be an altar. The table, then, is more than a piece of furniture for dispensing food. It is a focal point of the home where the family gathers for fellowship, for study of God's Word, and for prayer and blessing.

If you think that blessing is something that only priests or ministers can do, then consider the case of King David. He was not a priest; however, he often led Israel in worship. The Psalms are his offerings of praise and worship to God, songs that he sang to honor the Most High. On one occasion, David even led all of Israel in a spontaneous outburst of praise in which he "danced before the Lord with all his might" (2 Samuel 6:14). This was the time when David was moving the ark of the covenant to Jerusalem. David believed in corporate worship, and he led Israel in a spectacular demonstration of praise.

Listen, however, to what was the focus of David's attention at the end of this public worship experience. First, he "blessed Israel" (2 Samuel 6:18). Then, when "all the people went to their homes," David "returned home *to bless his household*" (2 Samuel 6:19-20, emphasis mine). Even though there were priests in Israel who were commissioned to bless the children of Israel, and even though he was the king of Israel, David still remembered that it was his responsibility as the leader of his household to bless his family in the sanctuary of their home!

What the ancient priests did in the temple, you can do in your home. You can pray, teach the Bible, and offer sacrifices of praise and thanksgiving, and you can also bless your family. What King David did in his home, you can do in yours. And God has made it easy for you. The blessings are all in the Bible, just waiting for you to employ them. You just can't go wrong using the inspired blessings in God's Word, because God's Word works!

How often should you bless your children? In Jewish tradition, all family blessings are given at least once each week (on the Sabbath). This is a special time when the family gathers around the table in the sanctuary of the home, shutting out everything else. It is an event that helps everyone understand the things that are really important in life: God and family.

You can profit from incorporating this Jewish tradition into your Christian home. Set a time once a week to gather your family around the family altar (the table). Share food, fellowship, prayer, Bible reading, and family blessings. Husbands, bless your wives. Wives, bless your husbands. Parents, bless your children. And let everyone bless God!

Why not demonstrate your faith by blessing your family? Surely, if it takes only a mustard seed of faith to move a mountain, we can muster enough faith to bless our children. Who knows, you too may be listed in the Hall of Fame of Faith because you took the time to bless your children "by faith" (Hebrews 11:20-21). When your children hear positive words of blessing, those words generate positive action in their lives. In addition, when you speak the Word of God over them, that Word generates faith unto salvation.

For the most positive results, a family celebration should be conducted in the home at least once a week as it is done with great success in Jewish homes around the world. Make sure you schedule a time for God and family. Otherwise, you will find it easy to forget or to postpone. Remember that nothing is more important to you than God and your family. Gather your family around the table, your family altar. Then, lead them in fellowship, study of God's Word, and prayer. Be sure to make this a time of blessing for your spouse and for your children. You can use the samples here, or you can create your own personalized blessings.

BLESSINGS FOR WIVES

Blessing your wife is important for your entire family: for you, for your wife, and for your children. You cannot speak the words of God's blessing over your wife if the words are not sincere and from your heart. Your wife will be blessed and esteemed in both her own eyes and as well as in yours. Finally, your children will see that you value and honor their mother. This builds their esteem for her and reinforces the feeling of the safety and stability of their home. This is why you should bless your wife in the presence of your children during your weekly family time.

The blessing that the Bible gives for wives is found in Proverbs 31:10-31. This blessing was taught to King Lemuel (probably Solomon) by his mother. It is even called a "prophecy" in Proverbs 31:1. According to Jewish tradition, Abraham spoke these words of blessing over his wife Sarah, and the prophetic words continued to be repeated generation after generation over the wives of his descendants. In some Jewish communities, husbands even sing this entire scriptural blessing to their wives each Sabbath evening.

You may use all or parts of this blessing:

"What a rare find is a capable wife! Her worth is far beyond that of rubies. Her husband puts his confidence in her and lacks no good thing. She is good to him all the days of her life. She looks for wool and flax and sets her hand to them with a will. She is like a merchant fleet, bringing her food from afar. She rises while it is still night, and supplies provisions for her household, the daily fare of her maids. She sets her mind on an estate and acquires it. She plants a vineyard by her own labors. She girds herself with strength and performs her tasks with vigor. She sees that her business thrives. Her lamp never goes out at night. She sets her hand to the distaff; her fingers work the spindle. She gives generously to the poor; her hands are stretched out to the needy. She is not worried for her household because of snow, for her whole household is dressed in crimson. She makes covers for herself; her clothing is linen and purple. Her husband is prominent in the gates, as he sits among the elders of the land. She makes cloth and sells it, and offers a girdle to the merchant. She is

A Blessing for Your Wife

What a rare find is a capable wife!
Her worth is far beyond that of rubies. Her husband
puts his confidence in her and lacks no good thing.
She is good to him all the days of her life.... She gives
generously to the poor; her hands are stretched out
to the needy.... Her husband is prominent in the gates,
as he sits among the elders of the land.... She looks to
the future cheerfully. Her mouth is full of wisdom, her
tongue with kindly teaching. She oversees the activities
of her household and never eats the bread of idleness.
Her children declare her happy. Her husband praises
her, "Many women have done well, but you surpass them
all." It is for her fear of the Lord that a woman is to be
praised. Extol her for the fruit of her hand, and let her
works praise her in the gates. In finding you I have found
happiness, and I have won the favor of the Lord.

clothed with strength and splendor. She looks to the future cheerfully. Her mouth is full of wisdom, her tongue with kindly teaching. She oversees the activities of her household and never eats the bread of idleness. Her children declare her happy. Her husband praises her, 'Many women have done well, but you surpass them all.' Grace is deceptive. Beauty is illusory. It is for her fear of the LORD that a woman is to be praised. Extol her for the fruit of her hand, and let her works praise her in the gates" (Jewish Publication Society *Tanakh*, a Hebrew translation).

You may want to add these words: "He who finds a wife has found happiness and has won the favor of the LORD" (Proverbs 18:22).

BLESSINGS FOR HUSBANDS

Blessing your husband is important for your entire family too. It is important for you, for your husband, and for your children. You cannot speak the words of God's blessing over your husband if they are not sincere and from your heart. By blessing your husband, he himself will be blessed, and he will be even more honored in his own eyes and yours. Finally, your children will see that you honor and respect their father, which will increase their esteem for him and help reinforce their sense that they are safe in their home.

Though it is not generally the tradition in most Jewish homes for a wife to bless her husband, wives can certainly bless their husbands with the words of Psalm 112:1-10 which virtually mirror the words of blessing outlined for wives in

A Blessing for Your Husband

Praise the Lord! Blessed is the man who fears the Lord,
who delights greatly in his commandments.
His descendants will be mighty on earth; the generation
of the upright will be blessed. Wealth and riches will be in
his house, and his righteousness endures forever.
Unto the upright there arises light in the darkness;
he is gracious, and full of compassion, and righteous.
A good man deals graciously and lends; he will guide his
affairs with discretion. Surely he will never be shaken;
the righteous will be in everlasting remembrance.
He will not be afraid of evil tidings; his heart is steadfast,
trusting in the Lord. His heart is established;
he will not be afraid. He has dispersed abroad,
he has given to the poor; his righteousness
endures forever; his horn will be exalted with honor.
In you I have found love and happiness
and the richness of God's blessing.

Proverbs 31. "Praise the LORD! Blessed *is* the man *who* fears the LORD, who delights greatly in his commandments. His descendants will be mighty on earth; the generation of the upright will be blessed. Wealth and riches will be in his house, and his righteousness endures forever. Unto the upright there arises light in the darkness; he is gracious, and full of compassion, and righteous. A good man deals graciously and lends; he will guide his affairs with discretion. Surely he will never be shaken; the righteous will be in everlasting remembrance. He will not be afraid of evil tidings; his heart is steadfast, trusting in the LORD. His heart *is* established; he will not be afraid. He has dispersed abroad, he has given to the poor; his righteousness endures forever; his horn will be exalted with honor."

You can speak this blessing over your husband in your family celebration.

BLESSINGS FOR CHILDREN

"And [Jesus] took the children in his arms, put his hands on them and blessed them" (Mark 10:16, NIV). One would think that this one sentence in the Bible would be enough to impress upon all Christians the importance of blessing children. For Jesus, however, this was much more than a casual, spontaneous act of compassion and love. It represented a rich and foundational part of his heritage as a Jew among his Israelite family and community.

For thousands of years, the Jewish people have regularly blessed their children, usually on a weekly basis. From the

JEWISH BLESSINGS FOR CHILDREN

Jewish fathers and grandfathers often stretch out their prayer shawls over children when they recite the words of the "Priestly Blessing."

time that Jewish children are babes in arms, their parents take full advantage of their weekly Sabbath family time to lay their hands on each of their children individually and to speak God's blessing into their lives. As this blessing scenario continues into adolescence and beyond, Jewish children simply grow up feeling blessed by their parents and by God.

Is it any wonder, then, that such a large percentage of them are so successful in life?

As we have noted, two of the earliest patriarchs of the Israelite community were recognized in the New Testament as an example of faith simply because they pronounced a blessing upon their children. Both Isaac and Jacob blessed their children "by faith" (Hebrews 11:20-21). Joseph actually brought his sons to their grandfather's deathbed so those same hands that years before had wrestled with the Lord could be placed upon their heads and they could receive a blessing in the same manner in which the patriarch had been blessed by the angel of the Lord at Peniel (Genesis 32:29; 48:9).

After David had fulfilled the responsibility of the King of Israel by restoring the ark, he retreated into the sanctuary of his own home "to bless his household" (2 Samuel 6:20). Is there any leader in either civil or religious circles who has a job more important than blessing his own children?

Nurturing in God's Instruction

Children need unconditional love and support. They need positive reinforcement. On a purely emotional level, regular and consistent blessing provides both. On a spiritual level, however, much more is accomplished when children are blessed by their parents. They are nurtured in God's instruction. The Word of God becomes real to them, not just some distant myth or legend. They actually experience for themselves what happened in Bible days. When you bless your children, you can even emphasize to children that you are doing the same thing that Jesus did.

God knew what he was doing when he commanded that his blessing be placed on the children of Israel throughout all their generations. Jesus was simply doing what he had seen the Father do when he took the children in his arms, laid his hands on them, and blessed them. Likewise, we who are God's children should imitate the life of Jesus. When we do, we are becoming more Christian (Christ-like). Jesus blessed the children. Do you want to be like Christ, a Christian indeed? Go and do likewise!

BLESSING FOR SONS

The Jewish people follow God's instructions by beginning their blessing for sons by saying, "May the LORD make you like Ephraim and Manasseh" (Genesis 48:20). The reason for their choosing these two is because they were the first brothers who put the welfare of the family and community over their own rights and did not fight one another over the birthright.

In the biblical Jewish tradition, it is proper to bless your son in this manner: Begin by laying your hand on his head and speaking the words that the Lord commanded the Israelites to say over their sons (Numbers 6:24-26): "The LORD bless you and keep you. The LORD cause his face to shine upon you and be gracious unto you. The LORD turn his face toward you and give you peace."

A Blessing for Your Son

The Lord bless you and keep you. The Lord cause his
face to shine upon you and be gracious unto you.
The Lord turn his face toward you and give you peace.
(In the tradition of Jacob who gave each of his sons
"the blessing appropriate to him," speak a personal blessing over
your son. This can come either from your own heart, or from
the blessings Moses spoke over the sons of Israel.)
May ther Lord make you like Ephraim and Manasseh.
May your mouth speak with wisdom. May your heart
meditate with reverence. May your hands do the work
that God has given you. May your feet hasten to follow
the path that God has laid out for your life.
May the Lord's full will for you be accomplished.
May the Spirit of the Lord, the spirit of wisdom and
understanding, the spirit of counsel and power, the spirit
of knowledge and the fear of the Lord be upon you.
May the grace of our Lord Jesus Christ, the love of God,
and the fellowship of the Holy Spirit be upon you
both now and forever.

Amen.

Next, you can speak a personal blessing over your son, expressing your own desires for his success and happiness. This is in keeping with the tradition of Jacob who blessed his twelve sons individually, "giving each the blessing appropriate to him" (Genesis 49:28).

You may also want to choose from among the blessings that Moses gave to the Twelve Tribes of Israel (Deuteronomy 33) those blessings that would be appropriate for your son:

"May you live long and abundantly before the LORD" [Reuben].

"May the LORD strengthen your hands and be a help to you whenever you call" [Judah].

"May the LORD bless all your skills and be pleased the works of your hands" [Levi].

"May you be beloved of the LORD and be protected by him" [Benjamin].

"May the LORD bless your land with all the precious gifts of heaven and earth, that you may give a great inheritance to your children" [Joseph for Ephraim and Manasseh].

"May God bless your works in the world, that you may draw others to God's mountain" [Zebulun].

"May God bless your home, that your sacrifices may end in abundance, and your house be filled with his treasures" [Issachar].

"May God choose the leader's portion for you, that you may carry out the LORD's righteous will in the land." (Gad).

"May you be ever like a young lion, protecting your family and defending justice for your people" [Dan].

"May you always be abounding in the favor of the LORD and in his blessings" [Naphtali].

"May you be favored of your brothers and sisters, and may your strength never fail you to the end of your days" [Asher].

You may also add these charges: "May your mouth speak with wisdom. May your heart meditate with reverence. May your hands do the work that God has given you. May your feet hasten to follow the path that God has laid out for your life."

You may then want to invoke the sevenfold Spirit of God upon your son: "May the Spirit of the LORD, the spirit of wisdom and of understanding, the spirit of counsel and of power, the spirit of knowledge and of the fear of the LORD be upon you" (Isaiah 11:2).

Finally, you may add this New Covenant benediction: "May the grace of our Lord Jesus Christ, the love of God, and the fellowship of the Holy Spirit be upon you both now and forever. Amen" (2 Corinthians 13:14).

BLESSINGS FOR DAUGHTERS

Jewish parents bless their daughters each week on the Sabbath by first invoking the words of blessing that the Israelites placed upon Ruth: "The LORD make you like Rachel and Leah" (Ruth 4:11), for it was these two women who "together built the house of Israel." You may use this blessing or say, "May the LORD make you like Sarah and Rebecca, like Rachel and Leah who together built God's household. May your entire life be fruitful, and may the LORD's full will for you be accomplished in your life."

Next, you will want to speak God's personal blessing over your daughter: "The LORD bless you and keep you. The LORD cause his face to shine upon you and be gracious unto you. The LORD turn his face toward you and give you peace."

Then, you can speak a personal blessing expressing your own desires for your daughter's success and happiness. This is in keeping with the tradition of Jacob who blessed his children individually, "giving each the appropriate blessing" (Genesis 49:28).

You may add these forms of blessing that were spoken of Ruth: "Blessed are you of the LORD, my daughter, for you have been kind and generous. The LORD God is your God, and his people are your people. May all the people know of certainty that you are a virtuous daughter" (Ruth 3:10; 1:16; 4:11).

You may also add these charges: "May your mouth speak with wisdom. May your heart meditate with reverence. May your hands do the work that God has given you. May your feet hasten to follow the path that God has laid out for your life."

You may also invoke the sevenfold Spirit of God upon your daughter: "May the Spirit of the LORD, the spirit of wisdom and of understanding, the spirit of counsel and of power, the spirit of knowledge and of the fear of the LORD be upon you" (Isaiah 11:2).

A Blessing for Your Daughter

The Lord bless you and keep you. The Lord cause his
face to shine upon you and be gracious unto you.
TheLord turn his face toward you and give you peace.
(In the tradition of Jacob who blessed each of his children with an
appropriate blessing, you may speak a personal blessing
over your daughter.)
Blessed are you of the Lord, my daughter, for you have
been kind and generous. The Lord God is your God,
and his people are your people. May all the people know
of certainty that you are a virtuous daughter.
May your mouth speak with wisdom. May your heart
meditate with reverence. May your hands do the work
that God has given you. May your feet hasten to follow
the path that God has laid out for your life. May your
entire life be fruitful. May the Lord's full will for you be
accomplished in your life. May the Spirit of the Lord, the
spirit of wisdom and understanding, the spirit of counsel
and power, the spirit of knowledge and the fear of the
Lord be upon you. May the grace of our Lord Jesus
Christ, the love of God, and the fellowship of the
Holy Spirit be upon you both now and forever.

Amen

You may want to say: "Blessed are you of the LORD, my daughter, for you have been kind and generous. The LORD God is your God, and his people are your people. May all the people know of certainty that you are a virtuous daughter."

Finally, you may add this New Covenant benediction: "May the grace of our Lord Jesus Christ, the love of God, and the fellowship of the Holy Spirit be upon you both now and forever. Amen."

CHAPTER 5

Blessings for Family Occasions

According to the Jewish tradition, there is virtually no event or circumstance in life that is not an occasion for a blessing of praise to God. Every life situation is also an opportunity for extending God's blessing to others through our prayers and benedictions.

This is in keeping with Paul's instruction: "Give thanks in all circumstances, for this is God's will for you in Christ Jesus" (1 Thessalonians 5:18, NIV). Except for giving thanks before meals, Christians often give little or no thought to stopping to thank God and to bless one another as the events of their lives unfold. Thankfulness and blessing should become an automatic response in the mind and heart of every believer.

If we adopt the mindset that King David had, we "will bless the LORD at all times" (Psalm 34:1). Out of our mouths will proceed blessings for God and for one another. When we begin to think in terms of blessing, we will find that it becomes the natural thing for us to do.

Most believers, however, have been robbed of this element of spiritual health. "Who am I?" they ask. "I'm not a pastor. I'm not a priest. I can't bless anyone." The reality is that every believer is a priest of God, a part of the priesthood of all believers (Revelation 1:6). As such, every believer is authorized and has a commission to bless others. God distributes his grace and gifts to everyone as he wills, and each divine empowerment is for the purpose of blessing the community of faith (Romans 12:6; 1 Corinthians 12:4).

It is time for every believer to reclaim this ancient biblical heritage of blessing and to begin to exercise it with all the vigor and confidence that comes with God-given authority. Every occasion that unfolds has tremendous potential for blessing, for speaking good words into the situation, into the lives of others, and unto the name of God.

We have outlined just a few of the circumstances in which you can bless your family with the blessing of God. You can be creative and think of many other events as well. Open your heart to the blessing impulse that is in your spirit, and you will be amazed to find that in all things you can bless the Lord. You can also touch the lives of loved ones and even total strangers as you become an instrument of God's grace and peace.

BLESSINGS AT MEALS

Christians generally bless their food before they eat, offering a short prayer to God. Interestingly enough, when God commanded Israel to give thanks at meals, he told

A Blessing Before a Meal

We bless your name, O Lord our God, Sovereign of the
universe, for the bounty of the earth and for the food
that you have created and so graciously provided
to strengthen and sustain our bodies.
May you bless our fellowship through the name of
your Son, Jesus Christ, our Lord.

Amen.

them to bless the Lord for their food after they had eaten:
"When you have eaten and are full, *then* you shall bless the
Lord your God for the good land which he has given you"
(Deuteronomy 8:10). This passage of Scripture is the source
for the oldest blessing that exists in the Hebrew tradition. It
is called the *Birkath HaMazon*, the blessing after the meal.
Maybe God thought it was easier to give thanks after one's
hunger was satisfied than to do so on an empty stomach!

Much later, the sages of Israel suggested that no food (or
anything else that is pleasurable) should be enjoyed without
first blessing God. They created blessings that honored God

for food and beverage that were to be spoken before meals. First, there was the blessing for the bread: "Blessed are you, O LORD our God, Sovereign of the universe, who brings forth bread from the earth." Then, there was the blessing for the fruit of the vine: "Blessed are you, O LORD our God, Sovereign of the universe, who creates the fruit of the vine."

In biblical tradition, one does not "bless the food." The blessing is given as an act of praise to the one who has given the food, the Lord himself. Food does not need to be blessed, because it was created by God and was proclaimed by God to be good. The concept that material things are evil is from Greek tradition that considered all matter evil. Some Christians came to believe that it was necessary to bless the things that they used in order to make them "holy." The prophets, Jesus, and the apostles consistently blessed the Lord with the ancient tradition that began, "Blessed are you, O LORD our God, Sovereign of the universe …"

It is virtually certain that Jesus spoke some form of these blessings at his meals. At the Last Supper, he "blessed" when he gave the bread to his disciples and when he shared the cup with them as well. Since the *Birkath HaMazon* after-meal blessing is the oldest practiced blessing in the Bible, it is also almost certain that Jesus and his disciples spoke the words of this blessing as well.

The blessing after the meal gives continuity to the evening of Sabbath blessing that the Jewish family celebrates each week. Many blessings are given before the meal (blessing children, wife, and God). After food is enjoyed, the *Birkath HaMazon* focuses the entire family's attention on God as

A Blessing After a Meal

Blessed are you, O Lord our God, Sovereign of the
universe, who feeds the whole world with your goodness,
with grace, with loving kindness and tender mercy.
Through your great goodness, we have never lacked for
food. Blessed are you, O Lord, who gives food to all.
We thank you, O Lord our God, because you have given
us a desirable, good, and ample land. We thank you for
the food wherewith you constantly feed and sustain us
every day, our daily bread. We bless your name
even as it is written: "You shall eat and be satisfied,
and you shall bless the Lord your God
for the good land which he has given you."
Blessed are you, O Lord, for the land and for the food.
Have mercy, O Lord our God, upon all your children,
and help us to remember that we need only your
helping hand as we trust your promises
through Jesus Christ, our Lord.

Amen.

the provider of food not only for themselves but also for the entire world. This blessing after the meal is given in the following manner:

The father says, "Let us say grace." The rest of the family responds, "Blessed be the Name of the LORD from this time forth and forever." The father continues, "We will bless him of whose bounty we have partaken." The family responds, "Blessed is he of whose bounty we have partaken and through whose goodness we live."

Then the family blesses God as the one who "feeds the whole world" and as the one from whom "we have never lacked food." Next, as the Lord commanded, the family blesses God "for the good land which [God] has given you." These blessings are a response to God's specific command in Deuteronomy 8:10-12). During the second century A.D., the Jewish people added a third petition to this blessing, asking God to "have mercy upon Israel, upon Jerusalem, upon the house of David, and upon the temple" and to ensure that they would "have need only of God's helping hand."

Jesus always blessed God and give thanks before he ate. He did so at the Last Supper. "Jesus took some bread and after a blessing, he broke it and gave it to the disciples, and said, 'Take, eat; this is my body'" (Matthew 26:26, NAS). "Then he took the cup, and *gave thanks* [blessed], and gave it to them, saying, Drink from it, all of you" (Matthew 26:27, NKJV).

Jesus blessed the Father (not the loaves and fishes) before he miraculously fed the multitudes. "Then he commanded the multitudes to sit down on the grass. And he took the five loaves and the two fish, and looking up to heaven, he *blessed* and broke and gave the loaves to the disciples; and the disciples gave to the multitudes." (Matthew 14:19, emphasis added).

Paul also instructed believers that they should continue this biblically Hebraic tradition in blessing God (giving thanks): "Every creature of God *is* good, and nothing is to be refused if it is received with thanksgiving" (1 Timothy 4:4).

BLESSINGS AT HOLIDAYS

Holidays are not just days off from work. They are, as the meaning of the word indicates, "holy days" designed by God to give us a chance to catch our breath from the hustle and bustle of life and remember the things that are of the greatest value to us: God and our families. This is especially true of those times that God has asked us to set apart on our calendars to remember the great events of salvation history.

In reality, God has made appointments on his own calendar to meet with his children and has invited us to set aside the other demands of life and meet with him at those times. These appointments include daily hours of prayer, weekly Sabbaths, seasonal festivals, and generational celebrations. Because it is so easy for us to forget, these appointments on our spiritual calendar help us to remember. They give us opportunity to draw close to God and to our families and friends, something that all too easily gets crowded out unless we take the time to schedule it. When we follow God's appointment calendar, our whole focus changes because we are constantly reminded of what is really important in life: God, our families, and our friends.

In a tradition of the Jewish people that was firmly in place during the time of Jesus and the apostles, a special prayer of blessing is prayed on holy days that focuses people's entire attention on the God of the universe. This prayer of blessing is called the *Amidah* because it is always spoken while standing (not sitting). It is so important that it is also called "The Prayer." If Jesus prayed this prayer (and it is virtually certain that he did when he shared worship with his Jewish family in temple and synagogue), it should have great value for Christians as well.

You will be blessed when you recite the following blessing prayer, for in doing so, you share in praying a 2,000-year-old prayer that was prayed by the biblical people, including our Lord Jesus and his disciples.

A Blessing Prayer for Special Occasions

An Edited Form of the Festival or Sabbath Amidah

(May Be Read Responsively)

O Lord, open our lips, and our mouths shall declare your praise.

Blessed are you, O Lord our God and God of our fathers, Abraham, Isaac, and Jacob; the great, mighty and revered

God, the Most High God, who bestows loving kindnesses, and is Master of all things; who remembers the pious deeds of the patriarchs, and in love will bring redemption to their children's children for your Name's sake.

O King, Helper, Savior, and Shield. Blessed are you, O Lord, the Shield of Abraham.

You, O Lord, are mighty forever, you revive the dead, you are mighty to save. You sustain the living with loving kindness, revive the dead with great mercy, support the falling, heal the sick, free the bound, and keep your faith to them that sleep in the dust. Who is like unto you, Lord of mighty acts, and who resembles you, O King, who orders death and restores life, and causes salvation to spring forth? Yes, faithful are you to revive the dead. Blessed are you, O Lord, who resurrects the dead.

We will sanctify your Name in the world even as they sanctify it in the highest heavens, as it is written by the hand of thy prophet: And they called one unto another and said,

Holy, holy, holy is the Lord of hosts: the whole earth is full of his glory.

Those over against them say,

Blessed be the glory of the Lord from his place.

And in thy Holy Word it is written, saying,

The Lord shall reign forever; your God, O Zion, unto all generations. Praise the Lord.

Unto all generations we will declare your greatness, and to all eternity we will proclaim your holiness. Your praise, O Lord our God, shall not depart from our mouth forever, for you are a great and holy God and King. Blessed are you, O Lord, the holy God.

You favor man with knowledge and teach mortals understanding.

You have favored us with knowledge of your Word and have taught us to perform your will. You have made a distinction, O Lord our God, between holy and profane, between light and darkness, between Israel and the nations, between the Sabbath and the six working days. O our Father, our King, grant that the days which are approaching us may begin for us in peace and that we may be withheld from all sin and cleansed from all iniquity and cleave to the reverence of your name.

Blessed are you, O Lord our God, who sanctifies Israel and the festive seasons.

Accept, O Lord our God, your people Israel and their prayer; restore the service to the inner sanctuary of your house; receive in love and favor both the offerings of Israel and their prayer; and may the worship of your people Israel be ever acceptable unto you.

Our God and God of our fathers! May our remembrance ascend, come, and be accepted before you, with the remembrance of our fathers, of Messiah the Son of David your servant, of Jerusalem your holy city, and of all your people, the house of Israel, bringing deliverance and well-being, grace, loving kindness and mercy, life and peace on this time of celebration.

Remember us, O Lord our God, thereon for our well-being; be mindful of us for blessing, and save us unto life: by your promise of salvation and mercy, spare us, and be gracious unto us; have mercy upon us, and save us; for our eyes are bent upon you, because you are a gracious and merciful God and King. Let our eyes behold your return in mercy to Zion. Blessed are you, O Lord, who restores your divine presence unto Zion.

We give thanks unto you, for you are the Lord our God and the God of our fathers for ever and ever; you are the Rock of our lives, the Shield of our salvation through every generation.

We will give thanks unto you and declare your praise for our lives which are committed unto your hand, and for our souls which are in your charge, and for your miracles, which are daily with us, and for your wonders and your benefits, which are wrought at all times, evening, morn, and noon. You who are all good, whose mercies fail not, you, merciful God, whose loving kindnesses never cease, we have ever hoped in you.

Grant peace, welfare, blessing, grace, loving kindness, and mercy unto us and unto all Israel, your people. Bless us, O our Father, even all of us together, with the light of your countenance; for by the light of your countenance you have given us, O Lord our God, the Word of life, loving kindness and righteousness, blessing, mercy, life, and peace; and may it be good in your sight to bless your people Israel at all times and in every hour with your peace.

Blessed are you, O Lord, who blesses your people Israel with peace.

O my God! guard my tongue from evil and my lips from speaking guile. Let the words of my mouth and the meditation of my heart be acceptable before you, O Lord, my Rock and my Redeemer. He who makes peace in his high places, may he make peace for us and for all Israel. Amen.

Blessings for Unborn Children

The formation of an unborn infant in the womb is not merely a biological accident. God is intimately involved in the development of every child from the moment of conception until birth. David remarked upon the amazing process that brings new life into the world: "For you [Lord] formed my inward parts; you wove me in my mother's womb. I will give thanks to you, for I am fearfully and wonderfully made … My frame was not hidden from you when I was made in secret, and skillfully wrought in the depths of the earth; your eyes have seen my unformed substance; and in your book

A Blessing for an Unborn Child

Blessed are you, O Lord our God, Sovereign of the universe. In your wisdom, you have chosen to bless us with the gift of a new life to add blessing to our marriage and to our home. Bless this new life with your loving care, and keep your hand of blessing upon (his/her) mother during this time of formation and in the hour of birth. We speak comforting words of blessing to this new life, saying, "You are blessed in the name of the Father, and of the Son, and of the Holy Spirit. Amen."

they were all written, the days that were ordained for me, when as yet there was not one of them" (Psalm 139:13-16). Solomon marveled at the fact that God forms everything, even the mysteries of life in the womb (Ecclesiastes 11:5).

Apparently the Scriptures confirm the fact that there is awareness on the part of an unborn child in the womb When Mary, the mother of Jesus, came to John the Baptist's mother, Elizabeth, with the news of the promised Messiah, Elizabeth exclaimed, "As soon as the sound of your greeting reached my ears, the baby in my womb leaped for joy" (Luke 1:44, NIV). One can reasonably assume that unborn infants have awareness in the womb. Certainly God's spoken Word is powerful even to those who do not understand those words.

Blessing an unborn infant is certainly proper for both parents. Blessings for the infant and prayers for safe birth are appropriate. You may speak this blessing over your unborn child, or you may create your own blessing and prayer. Both father and mother may give their own blessings.

BLESSINGS FOR NEWBORNS

The birth of every child should be a time for joy and celebration. Children should be the fruit of love confirmed by a life-long covenant between godly parents and God. This was God's design in creating marriage: "Has not [the LORD] made them one? In flesh and spirit they are his. And why one? Because he was seeking godly offspring" (Malachi 2:15).

A Blessing for Your Newborn Child

Blessed are you, O Lord our God, for the bounty of your
provision in our lives. We give you praise for the child you
have given us. Thank you that you have preserved his/
her mother's health. As you have commanded,
we bless this, your child with your own blessing:
The Lord bless you and keep you. The Lord cause his
face to shine upon you and be gracious unto you.
The Lord turn his face toward you and give you peace.
May the grace of our Lord Jesus Christ, the love of God
our Father, and the fellowship of the Holy Spirit be upon
you, my child, both now and forever. Amen.

Children are not an accident of nature: they are God's
gift. "Behold, children are a gift of the LORD; The fruit of
the womb is a reward" (Psalm 127:3, NAS). If they are indeed
God's reward to loving parents, then God should be praised
and blessed when they are received. It is highly appropriate
to speak words of blessing into the life of an infant, even the
words that God commanded to be spoken over the children
of Israel.

When Isaac was weaned, Abraham had a great celebration
(Genesis 21:8). This was an indication of the value that he

had for his son and of the gratitude that he had to God for his gift to Sarah and himself.

As a Christian believer, you understand that God has entrusted you with the life of your infant child. You have been assigned as a guardian with the responsibility of nurturing and instructing your child from infancy in the ways of God (Ephesians 6:4). You are responsible for providing food, clothing, and shelter for your child and for maintaining a secure environment of safety and blessing.

One way in which you can keep this responsibility foremost in your life is by blessing your child regularly, even weekly as the biblical peoples did. The time to begin to bless is even before the child is born!

Blessings at Graduations

Study and learning have always been considered sacred in the biblically Hebraic tradition. The Wisdom Books of Holy Scripture extol the virtue of acquiring knowledge, understanding, and wisdom (Proverbs 4:5). They also exhort young men and women to study God's Word and to do it with all diligence (Proverbs 1:4).

There is no biblical distinction between spiritual understanding and secular knowledge. All knowledge springs from God who breathes insight into the human heart and mind (Job 32:8). In the Hebraic tradition, therefore, a father is responsible for teaching his children the Word of God and for equipping them with a means of livelihood.

A Blessing for Your Graduate

God's Word gives you these words of
instruction and blessing:
Pursue instruction rather than silver.
Acquire knowledge rather than fine gold. Know wisdom
and understanding, justice, judgment, and equity.
How blessed are those who find wisdom and whose who
get understanding. Blessed are the ones who persevere
under trial because they will receive the crown of life.
Wisdom is the principal thing, therefore get wisdom.
And in all your getting, get understanding. Hold on to
instruction, do not let it go, keep it, for it is your life.
Whoever gives heed to instruction prospers,
and whoever trusts in the Lord is blessed.
May you always study to love and honor
the Lord your God, and may you be blessed
for doing so.

(Taken from Proverbs 8:10; 3:13-14; James 1:12;

Proverbs 16:20; 4:7, 13)

Both spiritual insight and secular understanding are essential to happy, healthy, and productive lives.

There is also a long-standing tradition among the Jewish people in which teachers blessed students. This parallels the blessing that parents give their children. It also underscores the importance that education and educators have in the lives of growing and maturing children. Parents are the first teachers. Then, others become stewards of the process of learning, adding knowledge, understanding, and wisdom in a clear parental role.

Graduations are important milestones that mark educational accomplishment. They are rites of passage from one level of knowledge and understanding to another and finally into a position where what has been acquired can be put to work to provide stable, secure, and joyful lives for families and communities. These blessings can be given at graduations from various levels of schooling.

BLESSINGS AT RITES OF PASSAGE

In ancient times and in many cultures, the time at which children reached puberty was considered an important event. Various rites of passage were used to mark this time of transition from childhood to adolescence.

In the Jewish culture, a long-standing practice has recognized this stage of development. For boys, it is called *Bar Mitzvah* (Son of the Commandment); for girls, it is called *Bat Mitzvah* (Daughter of the Commandment). For boys, it is at the age of thirteen; for girls it is at the age of

A Blessing for Your Child When Adolescence Begins

We will ever be thankful to God for blessing us by
entrusting us with your life. Now, we surrender you
into God's hands alone, to whom you are responsible
and accountable for your actions. We promise to love
and support you in the coming years as you grow into
adulthood. We bless you with the blessing that
God commanded for his children:
The Lord bless you and keep you.
The Lord cause his face to shine upon you and
be gracious unto you. The Lord turn his face toward you
and give you peace. May the Spirit of the Lord,
the spirit of wisdom and of understanding, the spirit of
counsel and of power, the spirit of knowledge and of
the fear of the Lord be upon you. May your mouth speak
with wisdom. May your heart meditate with reverence.
May your hands do the work that God has given you.
May your feet hasten to follow the path that God has laid
out for your life. May the grace of our Lord Jesus Christ,
the love of God, and the fellowship of the Holy Spirit
be upon you both now and forever.
Amen.

twelve. Originally the achievement of this status required no ceremony; however, in more modern times, ceremony and blessing have become a common institution in Judaism.

This is the time when a child assumes responsibility for his or her own actions. During the ceremony, the child normally says, "Today I am a man (or woman)." The child is invited to make *"aliyah"* by "going up" in the synagogue to recite the customary blessing over the weekly Scripture reading. This is also a time for public demonstration of the child's understanding of his or her faith and of the Word of God.

This practice is likely the source of the tradition among some Christians that children reach an "age of accountability," when they alone become responsible before God and society for their actions. There is no specific scriptural definition of the age at which this occurs; however, its connection with the onset of adolescence is certainly appropriate.

In many Christian communions, a similar experience is celebrated in Confirmation. This practice gives recognition of the child's accomplishment in understanding and commitment to Christian faith. Many fellowships, however, let this important time in a child's development pass with hardly any notice.

In a time when dramatic hormonal and physical changes are taking place in a child's life, it is very important that strong affirmation and commitment to God and his Word be manifest and that continuing parental support be affirmed for the decision-making process that the adolescent must begin to assume. At this time, a private family celebration or a public corporate exercise is certainly in order with appropriate blessings.

Blessings for Weddings

Weddings are among the most important events in life. Marriage was instituted by God in the beginning so that one man and one woman might be joined for life in a divine covenant of loving commitment to one another and to the family that they become. God has made the two to become one so that godly children might be brought into a secure and stable environment of love and support (Malachi 2:15). He has brought two parts of a whole together so that both may be complete, balancing and complementing each other (Genesis 2:24).

Various ceremonies have been developed by different cultures to formalize the covenant between bride and groom. Traditional Christian wedding ceremonies have begun with the father of the bride "giving" his daughter to be married to the groom. This practice, however, has come to be seen as a perpetuation of a longstanding belief that women were property owned by either their father or their husband, so this practice is rightly being abandoned.

A much better declaration has come to be added to the wedding ceremony in which the parents of both bride and groom offer their blessing upon the couple. This may be a simple response of "We do" to the minister's question, "Who blesses this marriage?" It may also be more involved with one or all parents speaking personal blessings into the lives

A Parent's Wedding Blessing for the Bride

What a rare gift is a capable wife! She is worth far more than rubies. May your husband put his full confidence in you and never lack anything of value. May you bring him good all the days of your life. May you always be strong and your health be vigorous so that you may watch over the affairs of your home. May your arms always be extended to the poor and the needy. May you be clothed with strength and dignity. May God give you wisdom, and may faithful instruction be always on your tongue. Many women have done well, but may you surpass them all. You have been a treasure to us, a gift and a heritage from the Lord. We are thankful that God entrusted us with your life and has allowed us to nurture you unto this time. As you now join with your beloved to create a new home, we bless you with all the blessings of heaven and earth. May the Lord answer you when you are in distress. May he remember your sacrifices and give you the desires of your heart. May you enjoy the fruit of your labor and may prosperity and blessing be yours. May the Lord bless you all the days of your life, and may you live to bless and enjoy your children's children.

A Parent's Wedding Blessing for the Groom

Blessed is the man who fears the Lord, who delights greatly in his commandments. The generations that follow you will be blessed because of your goodness.
May you be gracious to your wife and full of compassion. May you never be afraid. Let your heart always be steadfast, trusting in the Lord. May you always remember to give to the poor and conduct your affairs generously and with justice so that wealth and riches may be in your own house.
You have been a treasure to us, a gift and a heritage from the Lord. We are thankful that God entrusted us with your life and has allowed us to nurture you unto this time. As you now join with your beloved to create a new home, we bless you with all the blessings of heaven and earth.
May the Lord answer you when you are in distress. May he remember your sacrifices and give you the desires of your heart. May you enjoy the fruit of your labor and may prosperity and blessing be yours. May the Lord bless you all the days of your life, and may you live to bless and enjoy your children's children.

of their children. Whatever the case, this should be done tastefully in a supportive manner because the ceremony is for the bride and the groom. Options are as many and varied as the creativity of bride and groom and their parents.

The important part of this exercise is the solidarity of parental support for the creation of a new family and the giving of parental blessings upon their children in the tradition of the ancient Hebrews.

BLESSINGS FOR GRANDCHILDREN

Grandparents should always be welcomed to be a significant part of their grandchildren's lives, especially in blessing them in the name of the Lord. Solomon observed, "Grandchildren are the crown of the aged" (Proverbs 17:6). Just as grandparents are rightly proud of their grandchildren, so they should participate in blessing them as well. One of the reasons that God chose Abraham and blessed him was because he knew that Abraham would teach his children and his grandchildren the ways of the Lord (Genesis 18:19). Joseph considered it vitally important that his father bless his sons with the patriarchal grandfather's blessing: "Joseph said to his father, [these] are my sons, whom God has given me here. So [Jacob] said, Bring them to me, please, that I may bless them" (Genesis 48:9) Joseph even commanded that all Israel should be blessed with these words: "May God make you like Ephraim and Manasseh," Jacob's grandsons (Genesis 48:20).

Blessing for Grandchildren

Blessed are you, O Lord our God, Sovereign of the universe, who has blessed us with life to see your glory in our children's children. May you bless _____ with the abundance of your grace and peace, filling her/his heart with faith and commitment to justice and mercy. May you live to speak God's blessing into the lives of your children's children. The Lord bless you and keep you. The Lord cause his face to shine upon you and be gracious unto you. The Lord turn his face toward you and give you peace. In the name of the Prince of peace, Jesus Christ our Lord. Amen.

As a parent, you can honor your own parents by asking them to pronounce God's family blessing upon your children. When grandparents bless their grandchildren, they are participating in an ancient biblically Hebraic practice that honors grandparents, parents, and children alike. It affirms the biblical tradition of the transfer of wisdom and blessing from parent to children and then to grandchildren.

BLESSINGS FOR PARENTS

Solomon spoke of the time when a righteous woman's children would rise up to call her blessed: "A virtuous woman's price is far above jewels … her children rise up and bless her" (Proverbs 31:10, 28). Indeed, one of the Ten Commandments requires children to honor their parents (Exodus 20:12). It is, therefore, appropriate that when children have passed beyond adolescence and have become responsible for their own actions before God, they should bless their parents. Continual engagement in this exercise

A Blessing for Your Father

Blessed is the man who does not walk in the counsel of the wicked whose delight is in the law of the Lord and who meditates day and night in God's Word. Blessed is the man who fears the Lord, who greatly delights in his commandments. We thank you for the father that you have given us, and we rise up to call him blessed of the Lord. May you, Father, be blessed with long life and health and may you rejoice in the blessing of your children's children.
May the God of peace grant you his everlasting peace through Jesus Christ, our Lord. Amen.

will help children fulfill God's commandment and receive the reward of long life as a result. As they bless their parents in the name of the Lord, they will lovingly care for them in their advanced years and so fulfill the intent of God's instruction. Solomon required such blessing: "Listen to your father who gave you life, and do not despise your mother when she is old" (Proverbs 23:22).

You may recite the words of Psalm 1 or Psalm 112 over your father, or you may speak your own personal word of blessing. You may also recite Proverbs 31:10-28 over your mother, or you may personalize your own blessing for her.

A Blessing for Your Mother

The woman who fears the Lord is to be praised. She opens her mouth in wisdom, and the teaching of kindness is on her tongue. Strength and dignity are her clothing, and she smiles at the future. We thank you for the mother that you have given us, and we rise up to call her blessed of the Lord. May you, mother, be blessed with long life and health, and may you rejoice in the blessing of your children's children.

May the God of peace grant you his everlasting peace through Jesus Christ, our Lord. Amen.

BLESSINGS FOR HOMES

It was common in Bible days for people to bless their homes and the homes of others. Jesus instructed his disciples in this manner: "When you enter a house, first say, Peace be to this house" (Luke 10:5). This was not an unusual instruction though, for blessings were spoken by and upon the people of God on a regular basis. Jesus himself practiced his own instructions. When he appeared to his disciples after his resurrection, he greeted them by saying, "Peace be with you" (John 20:21).

It is especially appropriate for those who are moving into a new home or a different dwelling place to ask God's blessings upon their home. In the Jewish community, a blessing is spoken before a *mezuzah* is affixed to the doorpost of a new house or dwelling. This action is taken in literal obedience to God's commandment in Deuteronomy 11:20: "You shall write [my words] on the doorposts of your house and on your gates." (A *mezuzah* is a box that contains a parchment scroll that has God's commands in Scripture written upon it.)

You may speak God's words from Deuteronomy 11:18-26, you may speak the blessing below taken from this chapter, or you may speak your own personal blessing upon your house and upon your family.

A Blessing for Your Home

Blessed are you, O Lord our God, Sovereign of the
universe, who has commanded us to set apart our homes
as sanctuaries for fellowship in the Spirit,
for the instruction of your Word, and for prayer.
We hereby dedicate this dwelling place as a temple for
your Spirit and a habitation of peace. We invoke your
blessing upon our home and upon our family.
May you write your words on the very doorposts
of our home and empower us to teach them
to our children when we sit down in this house,
when we lie down, and when we rise up.
May you multiply our days and the days of our children
so that we may praise you in the land of the living.
We receive the blessing of your peace
as we walk in faith and observe your instructions.
May you ever make this dwelling a blessing of peace
in the name of Jesus our Lord.
Amen.

CHAPTER 6

Blessings for Everyone

In the tradition of the Holy Scriptures, believers can offer God's blessings and their prayers for everyone. Indeed, the command of God is that we pray for everyone everywhere: "Therefore I exhort first of all that supplications, prayers, intercessions, and giving of thanks be made for all men.... For this *is* good and acceptable in the sight of God our Savior, who desires all men to be saved and to come to the knowledge of the truth" (1 Timothy 2:1, 3-4). Jesus pronounces a blessing upon those who rejoice when they are persecuted (Matthew 5:10-12)! He even exhorts Christians to bless and pray for their enemies (Luke 6:28)!

Christians should keep themselves always in an attitude of blessing. James even wondered how it is possible for blessings and curses to come from the same fountain (James 3:9-10). Believers, therefore, should keep their hearts clean and their lips pure by learning to speak blessings to all in all situations. If, in every situation of life, Christians stopped to speak or pray a blessing, the world would change overnight!

79

Here are some blessings that you as a believer can use to bless everyone in your life.

BLESSINGS FOR LEADERS

As Christians, there are two kinds of leaders who impact our lives: spiritual leaders and civic leaders. As a part of the divine system of oversight and protection for humankind, leaders have been appointed by God for our own welfare and blessing. Throughout the Holy Scriptures, we are instructed to give proper respect to both kinds of leaders. This includes the responsibility to pray for our leaders and to bless them in the name of the Lord.

SPIRITUAL LEADERS

Believers are admonished in the Epistle to the Hebrews: "Remember your leaders, who spoke the word of God to you. Consider the outcome of their way of life and imitate their faith.... Obey your leaders and submit to their authority. They keep watch over you as men who must give an account" (Hebrews 13:7, 17, NIV).

God spoke these words to Moses concerning the spiritual leaders of Israel: "I myself have selected your fellow Levites from among the Israelites as a gift to you, dedicated to the LORD" (Numbers 18:6, NIV). Spiritual leaders are, therefore, God's gift of blessing to his people. It is only proper, then, that God's people should also bless their leaders and as Aaron and Hur did for Moses, by holding up their hands before the Lord, sharing the burden of leadership (Exodus 17:12).

A Blessing for Spiritual Leaders

We thank you, all-sufficient Father, for the provision
that you have made for our protection and well-being.
You have given as gifts to us the leaders who watch for
our souls and stand alongside us as guardians against the
powers of evil. We bless _____, whom you have
appointed to lead this community of faith.
May you ever guard and keep him/her in perfect peace
and may you strengthen him/her in the most holy faith.
Empower him/her to speak the truth in love. Like our
Lord Jesus Christ, may he/she keep all whom you have
committed into his/her care until the age to come. Amen.

CIVIL LEADERS

Paul has specifically instructed the church in this regard
about leaders in civil government: "Everyone must submit
himself to the governing authorities, for there is no authority
except that which God has established.... He is God's servant
to do you good.... Therefore, it is necessary to submit to
the authorities, not only because of possible punishment but
also because of conscience. This is why you pay taxes, for
the authorities are God's servants, who give their full time to
governing" (Romans 13:1,4-6, NIV).

Peter added this confirmation: "Submit yourselves for the Lord's sake to every authority instituted among men: whether to the king, as the supreme authority, or to governors, who are sent by him to punish those who do wrong and to commend those who do right" (1 Peter 2:13-15, NIV).

Daniel established this divine principle: God "changes times and seasons; he sets up kings and deposes them" (Daniel 2:21, NIV). Every power that exists is governed by God. He exalts and he removes leaders as it pleases him. It is for this reason that Paul admonished believers to pray for civil authorities: "I exhort first of all that supplications, prayers, intercessions, and giving of thanks be made for all men, for kings and all who are in authority, that we may lead a quiet and peaceable life in all godliness and reverence" (1 Timothy 2:1-2, NKJV).

Solomon expressed a great word of wisdom when he commanded: "Do not curse the king, even in your thought" (Ecclesiastes 10:20, NKJV). Daniel repeatedly expressed the same prayer of blessing both for the kings who had brought Israel (and himself) captive and the king who liberated Israel. He exclaimed to Nebuchadnezzar, Belshazzar, and Darius: "O king, live forever" (Daniel 3:9; 5:10; 6:6). If curses are inappropriate against civil leaders and if prayers should be offered for them, then surely blessings can be spoken over them and in their behalf.

Of course, many who live in some degree of oppression may want to say the blessing that the aged rabbi suggested for the Tzar in *Fiddler on the Roof*. Since there is a blessing

A Blessing for Civil Leaders

We honor you, O God, for your infinite wisdom in
providing leaders whom you have established to
protect the innocent and to punish the wicked.
We know that you establish authorities, setting the times
of their administration. We bless _____,
whom you have appointed to lead our society and
our community. May you give them wisdom in their tasks.
May they trust in you and uphold your law so that
the people of this community may live their lives in the
security of justice and peace. Amen.

for virtually everything in the Jewish community, he was
asked, "Is there a blessing for the Tzar?" The rabbi replied,
tongue in cheek, "May the Lord bless and keep the Tzar …
far away from us…." Some things that God asks cannot be
fully understood by the human mind. We must, therefore,
do what God said, expecting him to fulfill what we cannot
understand.

BLESSINGS FOR FRIENDS

There are many blessings that can be pronounced upon friends and fellow members of the community of faith.

First, you may want to adopt the practice of blessing as a form of greeting. This is what King Saul did when the Prophet Samuel came to visit him: Saul "went to meet him and to bless him." Your greeting may be a simple: "May God bless you," or it may take the form of the blessing that David said belonged to all of God's children: "The blessing of the LORD be upon you; We bless you in the name of the LORD" (Psalm 129:8).

You may wish to speak "The Blessing" into your friend or colleague's life by stretching forth your hand and saying, "The LORD bless you and keep you. The LORD cause his face to shine upon you and be gracious unto you. The LORD turn his face toward you and give you peace" (Numbers 6:24-26).

You may also wish to invoke the sevenfold Spirit of God upon your friend by saying, "May the Spirit of the LORD rest upon you, the spirit of wisdom and of understanding, the spirit of counsel and of power, the spirit of knowledge and of the fear of the LORD" (Isaiah 11:2).

Additionally, you may use any of the New Testament blessings, including these:

"May you prosper in all things and be in health, just as your soul prospers" (3 John 1:2).

A Blessing for Friends

The blessing of the Lord be upon you.
We bless you in the name of the Lord. May you prosper
in all things and be in health, and may your whole spirit,
soul, and body be preserved blameless at the
coming of our Lord Jesus Christ. May the grace of our
Lord Jesus Christ, the love of God, and the
fellowship of the Holy Spirit be with your forever.
Amen.

"May your whole spirit, soul, and body be preserved blameless at the coming of our Lord Jesus Christ" (1 Thessalonians 5:23, NIV).

"May the God of hope fill you with all joy and peace in believing, that you may abound in hope by the power of the Holy Spirit" (Romans 15:13, NIV).

"May the God of peace who brought up our Lord Jesus from the dead, that great Shepherd of the sheep, through the blood of the everlasting covenant, make you complete in every good work to do his will, working in you what is well pleasing in his sight, through Jesus Christ, to whom be glory forever and ever. Amen." (Hebrews 13:20-21).

"May the grace of our Lord Jesus Christ, the love of God, and the fellowship of the Holy Spirit be with you forever" (2 Corinthians 13:14).

You may also want to make a personal blessing upon your friend. The words that come from your heart are powerful and uplifting.

Whatever the case, look your friend in the eye, take them by the hand or lay your hand their head, and speak your heart and the words of inspiration that God gives you for them. They will be blessed, and you will be blessed, too.

BLESSINGS FOR STRANGERS

"Therefore love the stranger, for you were strangers in the land of Egypt" (Deuteronomy 10:19, NKJV).

"The LORD protects the strangers; He supports the fatherless and the widow" (Psalm 146:9, NASB).

"And sons of the stranger, who are joined to the LORD, to serve him, and to love the name of the LORD, to be to him for servants, every keeper of the Sabbath from polluting it, and those keeping hold on my covenant.... I have given to them in my house, and within my walls a station and a name better than sons and than daughters" (Isaiah 56:6, 5).

In ancient Israel, a strong tradition of hospitality and blessing toward total strangers was a part of the life of the community. God commanded the Israelites to bless the strangers among them because they had been strangers

A Blessing for Strangers

God of Abraham, Isaac, and Jacob,
we extend your blessing beyond the reaches of
our community of faith unto all the strangers around the
world. May you protect and bless them by your grace,
and may you give them a place in your house better than
that of sons and daughters. May you bring grace and
blessing upon us all through the tender mercies
of your Son, Jesus Christ.

Amen.

themselves in the land of Egypt. Even before that time, Abraham was a stranger in the Land of Promise when he left his family and crossed over the Euphrates River. This is why God instructed the Israelites to be hospitable toward strangers.

In a very real sense, all believers are pilgrims and strangers in the lands in which they live, for our "citizenship" is in heaven (Philippians 3:20), and like Abraham, we "look for a city that has foundations whose architect is God" (Hebrews 11:10). Because we are strangers, we are instructed to care for and bless strangers among us as well. Indeed, we can bless those whom we do not even know, because God's blessing is for everyone.

In the rich tradition of their Jewish ancestors, the apostles of Jesus encouraged Christians to extend hospitality and blessing to strangers. One of the requirements for the admission of widows to the support of the church was "if she has shown hospitality to strangers" (1 Timothy 5:10). John commended the Christians who "act faithfully" in showing kindness to others, "especially when they [are] strangers" (3 John 1:5). Hebrews 13:2 reinforced this rich Hebraic understanding: "Do not neglect to show hospitality to strangers." Then, it makes this startling observation: "… for by this some have entertained angels without knowing it" (NASB). We simply never know the extent to which God's blessing will come into our lives when we bless strangers.

Blessings for Enemies

In one of the most astonishing statements in Scripture, Jesus commanded, "Love your enemies, bless those who curse you, do good to those who hate you, and pray for those who spitefully use you and persecute you" (Matthew 5:44, NKJV). While others had understood God's commandment to love one's neighbor (Leviticus 19:18), some thought that it was proper to hate one's enemies (Matthew 5:43). Jesus underscored the fact that all human beings are God's children and, therefore, deserve God's love and the petition for his

A Blessing for Enemies

Almighty Father, we bless those who have cursed us.
Create a table of peace before us where we can
come and be reconciled to one another and to you.
Empower us to do good unto those who have
harmed us. We pray for them and for their spiritual
welfare. May you have mercy upon us all
through your Son, our Lord, Jesus Christ.

Amen.

blessing. Paul also instructed believers that they were to walk faithfully in the instructions of Jesus. Listen to his words: "When we are cursed, we bless; being persecuted, we suffer it; when we are slandered, we answer kindly" (1 Corinthians 4:12-13).

Paul's reiteration of the Son of God's commandment demonstrated what David meant when he said, "You prepare a table before me in the presence of my enemies" (Psalm 23:5). In the ancient culture, bringing enemies together to share food was a means of reconciling conflicts. So it is that God himself prepares a table before us for reconciliation between parties of a conflict when we understand that the Lord is our shepherd and that he leads us in paths of righteousness for his name's sake. When we have the courage to bless our enemies, God moves to bring justice and reconciliation.

BLESSINGS FOR THE WORLD

Christian believers are expected to pray for and to bless the entire world. This is because the fullness of the earth is the Lord's, including all its inhabitants (Psalm 24:1). This is very clear in the expression of God's gift of salvation to all humanity in the person of his Son Jesus: "For God so loved the world that he gave his only begotten Son, that whoever believes in him should not perish but have everlasting life" (John 3:16).

Since all in some dimension are God's children, the fruit of his labors of creation, he desires that his children avoid sibling rivalries and bring blessing and peace to one another in his name. This is why Paul strongly encouraged believers in this manner: "Therefore I exhort first of all that supplications, prayers, intercessions, and giving of thanks be made for all men … for this *is* good and acceptable in the sight of God our Savior, who desires all men to be saved and to come to the knowledge of the truth" (1 Timothy 2:1, 3-4).

You can have the satisfaction of pronouncing God's blessing upon everyone in the world and by so doing in effect bless the righteous and call the sinner to repentance and relationship with God. What would happen to the world

A Blessing for the World

Almighty God, Lord of heaven and earth,
we bless your name for all of your creation.
The fullness of the earth and its inhabitants belong
to you. We give you thanks that you have created all
humanity in your image and likeness for the purpose
of glorifying your Name in the earth. We extend your
blessing in petition for all men everywhere through our
supplications, prayers, and intercessions.
We pray that the blessing of salvation through
Jesus Christ our Lord will come unto all people
everywhere so that the knowledge of the glory of the
Lord will cover the earth as the waters cover the sea.
May you, the God of peace, bring the blessing of
peace to all the earth. May there truly be
peace on earth, good will to men through the name of
your son, the Prince of Peace,
Jesus Christ, the Lord.

Amen.

if every Christian followed in the footsteps of Abraham of old and became an intercessor for blessing upon all men everywhere, even including those who are evil and deserve God's judgment (as in the case of his intercession with God for Sodom and Gomorrah)?

This kind of attitude and action is in context with John 3:17: "For God sent not his Son into the world to condemn the world, but that the world by him might be saved." God's design is that all the families of the earth should be blessed through the faith of Abraham that was perfected and extended to all men by the death and resurrection of Jesus. Can we do less than bless everyone in the name of the Lord?

CHAPTER 7

Other Blessings

here are almost limitless occasions for blessings. The opportunities are myriad, for virtually every situation in life calls for a blessing of thanksgiving to be extended to God and for blessing to be spoken into the lives of others and into human circumstances. Once you have come to understand the biblical importance of blessing, you will begin to look for occasions for blessing, and you will be amazed at the number of events and circumstances in which the blessing of God will come to your mind. You can be quite inventive, for as a child of Abraham, God has called you to be a prophetic intercessor for blessing.

We have observed many situations in which you can be one who blesses others either by speaking blessing directly or by praying God's blessing indirectly, yet there can be many more.

TEACHERS' BLESSINGS FOR STUDENTS

It was common in biblical communities for teachers to bless their students during the course of the learning process.

A Teacher's Blessing for Children

Blessed are you, O Lord our God, Sovereign of the
universe, who has commanded us to bless your children.
We give you thanks for children whose hearts
are inclined toward you and who seek knowledge,
understanding, and wisdom that you freely give
to all those who seek your face. May you give
these children (or child's name) the guidance of
your hand and the protection of your grace as we
speak the words of the blessing you commanded, saying,
"The Lord bless you and keep you.
The Lord cause his face to shine upon you and
be gracious unto you. The Lord turn his face
toward you and give you peace."
In the name of the Prince of Peace,
Jesus Christ, our Lord.

Amen.

Rabbis would bless their *talmidim* (disciples) with the same blessing that the priests spoke over those who made offerings at the temple and that parents spoke over their children in the home.

In whatever setting, whether kindergarten, elementary, middle school, high school, or college, instructors assume the extended role of parents to the children who have been entrusted into their care for the learning process. In Hebrew, the words for parent (*horeh*), teacher (*moreh*), and instruction (*torah*) all come from the same root word (*yarah*), which literally means to aim an arrow at a target and hit it. Parents teach their children in infancy and in childhood and then entrust them to teachers for specialized learning to enrich their children's lives with knowledge, understanding, and wisdom and to extend and further fulfill parental responsibility for children's education. Teachers, therefore, can also participate in the parental responsibility for blessing their children by speaking words of blessing over them in the educational setting.

Community/Congregational Blessings

Ministers and congregational leaders have been gifted by God and recognized by communities to provide instruction in righteousness, leadership in worship, and inspiration in both Word and Spirit for the members of the community. In the capacity of biblical servant leadership, they are commissioned like the Levites of ancient times to "serve the services that serve" (Numbers 8:25). These include leading

A Community Blessing

Blessed are you, O Lord our God,
Sovereign of the universe, who has commanded us
to bless your children with your divine blessing.
In obedience to your Word, we bless by saying,
"The Lord bless you and keep you. The Lord cause his
face to shine upon you and be gracious to you.
The Lord turn his face toward you and give you peace."
May the God of peace, who brought up from the dead
the great Shepherd of the sheep
through the blood of the eternal covenant,
even Jesus our Lord, equip you in every good thing
to do his will, working in us that which is
pleasing in his sight, through Jesus Christ, our Lord,
to whom be glory forever and ever.

Amen.

the community in corporate worship through the teaching of the Word and the liturgy of worship. (The word *liturgy* literally means "the service of the people" and as such indicates that the systematic exercise of worship is an act of all the people and not just of a minister or leader.)

The act of blessing is a significant part of the corporate prayer and worship of the community of faith. In this case, the leader of the community is given responsibility to bless the congregation. The blessings can be many and varied; however, the most important blessing is *"The Blessing,"* for God established the Levitical system specifically for the purpose of blessing the people of Israel with this blessing. Other blessings may be added or spoken at any time and in any sequence; however, the Aaronic Benediction should be the most prominent form of blessing.

BLESSINGS WHEN PARTING COMPANY

As Shakespeare said, "Parting is such sweet sorrow!" When we must separate from loved ones and friends, we do so reluctantly, for we value and cherish the company of those who are dear to us. Our sorrow is lessened, however, by the expectation that we shall meet again, whether soon or in a time not yet known to us.

Since there is a blessing for virtually everything in the Bible, then surely there must be a blessing for parting company as well. And so there is. It is found in the words of blessing and petition that Jacob offered when he and his

A Parting Blessing

I know whom I have believed and am convinced
that he is able to guard what I have entrusted unto him.
I pray that you may prosper in all things and be in health,
even as your soul prospers. The name of the Lord is a
strong tower. We run to him, and we are safe.
May the Lord keep watch between you and me
when we are away from each other.

Mitzpah!

family were leaving the company of his father-in-law Laban. "May the LORD keep watch between you and me when we are away from each other"(Genesis 31:49, NIV). These words were all the more powerful and poetic when Jacob named the place where they were standing "*Mitzpah,*" which in Hebrew means "Watchtower." It was as though the patriarch were asking God to stand as a guard in a watchtower looking over both departing families until such a time as they would come together again. Only the all-seeing eye of the Shepherd of Israel could look in both directions at the same time to any distance to guard both parties as they went their separate ways.

The Hebrew word *mitzpah* can also indicate the punishing of a trespasser. God is the one who watches over his children and keeps them from the trespasser, from the devices of *Satan*, whose name means "the trap setter." When someone or something attempts to interfere, breaking the fellowship of those who trust in the Lord, he delivers them from the evil one and establishes their goings.

Until this day, parting Jewish families and individuals often speak simply one word in Hebrew, "*Mitzpah*," ("Watchtower,") understanding that God is the one who "watches between you and me when we are away from each other." In exchange of mail or email, Jews often use this one-word blessing: "*Mitzpah*."

The believer who knows whom he has believed is convinced that God is able to keep what he has committed unto him for that day (2 Timothy 1:12). "The name of the LORD is a strong tower; the righteous run to it and are safe" (Proverbs 18:10).

BLESSINGS FOR THE BEREAVED

In our human situation, we always look on the finality of death with sorrow. We are suddenly, and often without warning, separated by death from the company of someone we loved. We grieve at our loss. Though we try our best, we cannot escape the fact that it is appointed unto all human beings to die (Hebrews 9:27). The one thing that is certain about human life is that one day, it will end.

Death is the great equalizer. It comes to all men, rich and poor, powerful and helpless. At a time of bereavement, the Jewish people follow the example of Job who sat on the ground and was silent before the Lord (Job 1:20). At the same time, however, they recognize that God is to be blessed in all things, even in the pain and sorrow of death. For centuries at the time of the death of a loved one, they have also prayed the *Kaddish*, which is a prayer of praise to God and hope of the resurrection, not an act of mourning for the dead.

This is true also for Christians. As Paul said, "About those who have died ... grieve not as others who have no hope. For if we believe that Jesus died and rose again, even so God will bring with him those who sleep in Jesus" (1 Thessalonians 4:13-14). While everyone experiences grief at the passing of a loved one, those who have faith in the God of the Bible know that death is not the end but another step toward resurrection and eternal life.

When we follow the biblically Hebraic tradition, we understand that blessing is not something that is reserved only for the good things that happen in life. It is equally appropriate in reaction to those things that are or seem to be bad. This is true of death and bereavement as well as of life. As a matter of fact, the Scriptures suggest that the day of death is better than that of birth (Ecclesiastes 7:1).

When David declared, "I will bless the LORD at all times; his praise shall continually be in my mouth" (Psalm 34:1, NASB), he did not exclude the sorrows that life brings. He understood that God is sovereign over all and, like Paul, he believed that "all things work together for good to them that love God" (Romans 8:28).

Job understood this biblical principle and may well have set the example for the tradition that follows until this day among the Jewish people when he said: "The LORD has given, and the LORD has taken away. Blessed be the name of the LORD" (Job 1:21). Job had just experienced the savage attack of Satan against his family and his fortune. All was lost. He was alone, destitute, and afflicted with boils from head to toe. Could any misery have been worse?

Job had the wisdom to recognize that God was the source of everything that he had possessed, and he had the courage to praise and bless the Lord even in the disaster that had befallen him. He trusted that God was in control and that everything would take place according to God's purposes for his life.

Job also knew that even death was not final. "I know that my Redeemer lives, and that in the end he will stand upon the earth. And after my skin has been destroyed, yet in my flesh I will see God; I myself will see him with my own eyes–I, and not another" (Job 19:25-27, NIV). Job believed in the resurrection at the last day: "For there is hope for a tree, if it is cut down, that it will sprout again, and that its tender shoots will not cease. Though its root may grow old in the earth, and its stump may die in the ground, yet at the scent of water it will bud and bring forth branches like a plant.... Oh, that you would hide me in the grave, that you would conceal me until your wrath is past, that you would appoint me a set time, and remember me! If a man dies, shall he live again? All the days of my hard service I will wait, till my change comes. You shall call, and I will answer you" (Job 14:7-9, 13-15 NKJV).

Paul understood that death had been conquered forever by the resurrection of Jesus: "Death is swallowed up in victory … O Death, where is your sting? … Thanks be to God, who gives us the victory through our Lord Jesus Christ" (1 Corinthians 15:54-55, 57). He boldly declared, "For if we believe that Jesus died and rose again, even so God will bring with him those who sleep in Jesus.… For the Lord himself will descend from heaven with a shout, with the voice of an archangel, and with the trumpet of God. And the dead in Christ will rise first. Then we who are alive and remain shall be caught up together with them in the clouds to meet the Lord in the air. And thus we shall always be with the Lord. Therefore comfort one another with these words" (1 Thessalonians 4:14,16-18 NASB). As believers in Jesus and in the power of his resurrection, we are assured that if and when our bodies cease to function and surrender to death, we already have another body like the glorious body of Jesus (Philippians 3:21) prepared and waiting for us in the heavens (2 Corinthians 5:1). It is not something that will be created for us at some point in time in the future. It is already a reality, and the time will come when we will "be clothed upon with our body which is from heaven" (2 Corinthians 5:2).

For those who believe in the God of creation, death is merely a step into everlasting life. God is the God of the living, and he will give everlasting life to all who believe and receive the blessing of his priceless gift, his only begotten Son

A Blessing for the Bereaved

The Lord gives, and the Lord takes away:
Blessed be the name of the Lord. I know whom
I have believed and am persuaded that he is able
to keep what I have committed unto him until the
day of his coming. For the Lord himself will descend
from heaven with a shout, with the voice of an archangel,
and with the trumpet of God, and the dead in Christ
will rise. I know that my Redeemer lives and that
in the end he will stand upon the earth and in my flesh I
shall see him. O death, where is your sting?
O grave, where is your victory?
Blessed be the name of the Lord
who gives us the victory through
our Lord Jesus Christ.

Amen.

(John 3:16). If we believe this truth, we can bless the Lord in all things and trust him for life to come in the resurrection.

The Epistle to the Hebrews gives us this benediction: "Now may the God of peace who brought up our Lord Jesus from the dead, that great Shepherd of the sheep, through the blood of the everlasting covenant, make you complete in every good work to do His will, working in you what is well pleasing in His sight, through Jesus Christ, to whom be glory forever and ever. Amen" (Hebrews 13:20-21).

CHAPTER 8

Contending for Blessing

From a Hebraic perspective, prayer is more an action of conforming ourselves to God's will than a means of inducing God to fulfill our desires. It is an exercise in submitting to God's design, not an on-demand valet service. God is the source of our unknown and unperceived need (which is often contrary to what we think we need), and prayer is the means of communicating to God our willingness to receive what God knows we need. God is definitely not the great genie in the sky anxiously awaiting someone to stroke his bottle. It is important, therefore, that we understand how prayer helps us to rightly contend for God's blessing in our lives.

RECONFIRMING THE BLESSING

God's blessing is promised to all the children of Abraham. This is a simple and undeniable truth. God swore that he would fulfill his covenant with Abraham's children throughout all their generations forever (Hebrews 6:13). While Abraham knew that the blessing was secure from the first moment that God had spoken it to him, he frequently approached God for reconfirmation of that blessing. As he and his wife Sarah grew older, they turned to God in an outpouring of emotion because God's promise that they would have a son had not yet been fulfilled. God did not rebuke them for "unbelief." Instead, he embraced them in his grace and reconfirmed the covenant and the promise (Genesis 18:14).

Many years later, Abraham's grandson, Jacob, wrestled with his own fears that the promise that had been given to his grandfather would fail in his generation. He feared that his brother Esau would have him killed. He had heard God reconfirm the covenant and the promise as he viewed the angels on the ladder stretching from heaven to earth, but, being human, he needed his own personal encounter with God. He needed a fresh impartation of personal blessing. Jacob had lived under the cloud of being a supplanter, which was the meaning of his name (Genesis 25:26). He had received his brother Esau's birthright from their father Isaac through deception. He needed reassurance that he truly was God's choice in the matter of inheritance and blessing. The one who had received the spectacular vision of heaven now needed an earthly encounter.

When Jacob came to the point of crossing the Brook Jabbok, he knew that his life would change dramatically and that there was even a possibility that he would not survive. It was during this night of decision that Jacob "wrestled with the Lord." Perhaps Jacob joined with the Lord in contending with his own fears, for he needed divine assistance in overcoming his doubts. Whatever the case, Jacob contended for the blessing and would not release the "angel" until he had received the divine blessing. "I will not let you go until you bless me," he declared (Genesis 32:26). His determination to contend for the blessing resulted in a new identity when the blessing came: thereafter Jacob, the supplanter, was called "Israel," a prince with God (Genesis 32:28).

This is a clear example for prevailing prayer where we wrestle with ourselves and with God in the face of deep-seated need. God will never reject us when we engage him with such passion and intensity. Though the encounter with the Divine may leave us handicapped in some area of our lives, it will ever establish our resolve to believe God and to walk in the expectation of his realized promises. After Jacob wrestled with God, he walked with a limp, the evidence that he had engaged the Divine; however, he also walked in confidence that what God had promised, he would do.

But, this face-to-face encounter with God was not the end of God's blessing for Jacob. Some time later when he returned to Bethel, the place of his original vision, God appeared to him and "blessed him," repeating the promises that he had made to his grandfather, Abraham (Genesis 35:9). The covenant and the blessing were reiterated, reestablished, and reconfirmed. God was ever present to reassure Jacob of his support in every life situation that he encountered.

Believers today, like Jacob of old, often need to have God's promise and blessing reconfirmed. This is not a manifestation of unbelief. It is simply a human need to be reassured in the face of a new encounter or a new challenge. Life is a series of such events where we face the threat of the unknown. Though we know we are in covenant with God, we need reconfirmation of the blessing from the God who is ever present.

If God visited Abraham and Jacob repeatedly to reconfirm his covenant and blessing for them, he will do the same for all of his children. Abraham was blessed before he left Haran (Genesis 12:13); he was blessed after the binding of Isaac (Genesis 22:17); and when all was said and done, God "had blessed Abraham in all things" (Genesis 24:1). Abraham's life was an unfolding of continuous blessing. When he was at his lowest ebb, God came to him to reconfirm the blessing. And God will do the same for all of his children who come to him for reassurance and confirmation.

BLESSING THROUGH PETITION

It is proper for individuals to approach the heavenly Father as his children, seeking his favor and the impartation of his blessing. A prominent example is recorded in Psalm 67:1 where David offered this form of the Aaronic benediction as a petition for blessing: "God be merciful unto us, and bless us; and cause his face to shine upon us" (Psalm 67:1). This was a prayer seeking God's blessing by turning his face toward his people. David added this blessing to a song to remind the people that God's blessing was ever with them, and these words have been part of a song in Israel ever since his time, for the Psalms were and remain the Bible's hymnal as well as the source of many of its prayers.

Another example of contending for blessing is found in the prayer blessing of Jabez. Though he was rather obscure character in Scripture, Jabez was bold to offer these words of petition: "O that you would bless me indeed and enlarge my border, and that your hand might be with me, and that you would keep me from harm that it may not pain me!" (1 Chronicles 4:10). In this case Jabez requested a personal blessing for himself, exclaiming his hope that God would bless him by bringing both physical and spiritual benefits to him. First he hoped that God would expand the range of his possessions. Then he prayed that God would keep him from suffering. Is this not the very center of petition in the Lord's Prayer: "Give us this day our daily bread ... and deliver us from evil" (Matthew 6:11, 13)?

Is a blessing petition too bold or self-centered? Would God accept such a petition for self-blessing and grant it? The answer is found in Scripture itself: "God granted [Jabez] what he requested" (1 Chronicles 4:10). The boldness of Jabez' request was merely part of the continuing personal relationship that the Hebrew people had with God. They came into his presence with "reverent boldness" (Hebrews 4:16). While the biblical people had the highest respect for the honor of God the King, they also viewed him as their Father, one who would welcome them into his presence as a father would open his arms to his children. Indeed, one of the ancient prayers still prayed in today's synagogues begins with these words: *"Avinu, Malkenu"* ("Our Father, our King").

The Bible recounts several instances where leaders of Israel had the nerve to engage God in dialogue and even to argue with him. Such was the case of Abraham who negotiated with God over the destiny of Sodom and Gomorrah (Genesis 18:22-33). Likewise Moses argued with God over the fate of the rebellious Israelites, even requesting that if God were settled on destroying Israel, he would destroy the prophet first (Exodus 32:32).

Jesus himself underscored the nature of prayer in the illustration of the widow and the unjust judge, noting that the judge granted the widow's petition simply because her persistence got on his nerves! The Master concluded that if such an unjust judge would answer the widow's unrelenting petition, how much more would the heavenly Father grant the prayers of his children (Luke 18:5).

This is why the writer of Hebrews urges all believers to "come boldly unto the throne of grace, that we may obtain mercy, and find grace to help in time of need" (Hebrews 4:16). The word *boldly* is *parresia* in Greek and means "frankly, with fearless confidence." There is, therefore, no hint of reservation that should be exercised when approaching "the throne of grace" to seek God's blessing of grace and mercy. We can have both humility and boldness at the same time when we are petitioning the Almighty.

A Blessing of Petition for Divine Protection, Provision, and Personal Concerns

Almighty God, be merciful unto us and bless us,
and cause your face to shine upon us.
We come boldly unto your throne of grace,
that we may obtain mercy and find grace to help
in our time of need. Help us to know before whom we
stand and to examine our hearts and purpose to follow
your will for our lives. Bless us indeed, that your hand
might be upon us, and keep us from harm. Give us today
our daily bread. We will never cease to seek your face
until you bless us with your tender mercies. We are the
children of your covenant through Jesus Christ our Lord;
therefore, we believe that you will give us
the desires of our heart as they accomplish your will.
Accept our petition of praise as we exalt your name,
Most High God.
Amen.

Self-blessing?

Is it possible for us to bless ourselves? The very idea sounds outrageous; however, one passage of Holy Scripture says that we can. In comparing the blessing of God upon those who are obedient to his Word with the curse that is upon the disobedient, God himself says prophetically that the time will come when "whoever blesses himself in the land shall bless himself by the true God" (Isaiah 65:16). Apparently God recognizes and honors self-blessings that are based in blessing by the true God or by the truth of God. Perhaps this was the underlying nature of the exercises of both David and Jabez when they exclaimed in God's presence, "Bless us!"

Blessing oneself is not merely the mindless repetition of religious words and phrases. It is the exercise of pure faith in the words of the living God. Jesus promised his disciples, "Everything you ask or pray for, believe that you have it already, and it will be yours" (Mark 11:24). The key is to bless yourself by the God of truth, so conforming your desires to the will of God that what you seek is what God already wants for you. Even though asking a blessing upon ourselves may seem self-serving, it is in reality a demonstration of dependence upon God and of faith in him and his Word. As Jesus promised, when we seek God's kingdom first, all the material benefits that God has prepared for his servants will be added to us (Mathew 6:33).

When we bless ourselves through petition we must be careful that we are blessing ourselves in God and his truth. To do otherwise is to invite disaster and perhaps even a curse.

Because the heart of man is deceitful (Jeremiah 17:9), we must be careful with self-blessings, for they can be exercised through the imagination of our hearts in defiance of God's manifest will (Deuteronomy 29:19). We can ask amiss to consume it upon our own lusts (James 4:3). When the heart clearly conforms to God's Word, however, blessing ourselves through petition for favor is honorable and pleasing to God.

Praying God's Word

One of the greatest secrets to successful prayer is praying God's Word. We cannot pray amiss when we pray the Word, for God's Word is infallible. The Jewish people have long understood this secret as evidenced by the fact that virtually all of their corporate prayers and affirmations are either quoted or paraphrased Holy Scripture.

It has been suggested that God, like men, enjoys hearing the sound of his own voice, particularly when that voice takes the form of the declaration of his Word from the lips of his children. The Word of God forms in our hearts the faith that is the substance of what is not seen (Hebrews 11:1). We can be sure that we are not praying words of selfish lust when we pray the words of Holy Scripture. God's Word is alive and powerful (Hebrews 4:12). It is active and creative. It changes our hearts when it passes through them, and it opens our hearts to receive the blessing that God intends (even though it may not be the ones we have imagined).

Praying God's Word is yet another part of the Christian's Hebraic heritage, that enriching connection with the book, the history, and the culture of God's chosen people. Imagine what great blessing awaits you when you dare to be reconnected to the root system (Romans 11:17) of God's family tree of salvation and covenant relationship (the olive tree)!

Petitioning for Blessing

Jesus also made it clear that if a child of the kingdom asks the heavenly Father for bread, he will not be given a stone and that if he asks for fish, he will not be given a serpent (Matthew 7:9-10). Anyone who comes to God must believe that God exists and that God rewards those who diligently seek him (Hebrews 11:6). We know this for certain because Jesus Christ is the same yesterday, today, and forever (Hebrews 13:8). We have an advocate with the Father who is touched with our deepest need (1 John 2:1; Hebrews 4:15). Jesus will never drive away anyone who comes to him in faith (John 6:37). He is always filled with compassion (Matthew 14:14), and he stretches forth his hand of blessing to those who approach him in faith.

The boldness to petition God for blessing upon ourselves is well within our entitlements as believers; however, we often have not because we ask not or because we ask amiss (James 4:3). We must understand clearly that we always have access to God's throne through Jesus Christ and the completed work of Calvary. With this right of entrance into the heavenlies through prayer, we can position ourselves before the throne of grace and receive the impartation of blessing into our lives even as we speak that blessing in words of faith in God's provision (Hebrews 4:16).

Just as little Jewish children are taught to approach their parents with heads bowed for the impartation of the divine blessing, so believers should come boldly, yet reverently into their Father's presence expecting and receiving the reconfirmation of his promise and blessing. He will welcome them with open arms, place his hand upon them, and speak his everlasting benediction into their lives. When we contend for the blessing, we can be certain that he will give it to us in inconceivable dimensions. We already have his assurance that we need only ask, and we will receive. It's really that simple!

Chapter 9

Releasing God to Bless

ow can we be certain that God is free to bless us in every way that is according to his will? Are there obstacles that hinder us from being blessed? Can we discover the biblical secret of releasing God to bless everything that we put our hand to do?

The answer is so simple that it is too simple. God is our source. God's will is that we should be blessed beyond all measure of our own expectations. He is able to do exceedingly abundantly above all we are able to ask or think (Ephesians 3:20). In order for God to bless, however, we must recognize that we are completely dependent upon God's provision for his sustenance. We prove that God is our source by returning to him what he asks of us in tithes and offerings.

God has designed it so that when we give him the tenth (tithe) of our gain, it is as though we have given him everything. The Hebrew word for tithe, *mesher*, means both "a tenth" and "a very large amount, abundance, or wealth." When we give the tenth, we demonstrate to God that we are giving all. We do not seek to hold on to what we have gained as though we had acquired it through our own strength or as though we were afraid to part with any of it. We give back to God what he requires because we know he has given us all that we have.

The act of tithing is the mechanism that releases God to bless us. God specifically says this in his Word: "Bring the whole tithe to my storehouse.... Test me in this ... and see if I will not open the floodgates of heaven and pour out so much blessing that you will not have room enough for it" (Malachi 3:10). God promises that if we fully tithe, the floodgates of heaven will open with amazing blessings.

Too often Christians have been confronted with the issue of tithes from a negative standpoint. They have been told by church authorities of the curses that will come upon them if they fail to tithe. Church bureaucracies have insisted that their treasuries are "God's storehouse" and that all the tithe must come into either their local congregation or into their denomination. This negative approach has made tithing seem like a burden and a curse—like paying taxes! As a result many Christians either do not tithe at all or they do so begrudgingly. And we know if we give grudgingly, we miss the blessing!

The tithe is designed by God to provide a divine vehicle for blessing. "Give, and you shall receive," Jesus said (Luke 6:38). The first blessing is to the one who gives, to the tither. By obeying God's command, we release God to bless. The second blessing is to those who receive the tithe. This may be our local congregations or it may be ministries that are enriching our lives and the lives of others. It may also be our giving to the underprivileged of society and to other humanitarian causes.

It is the wisdom of God for us to sow the seed of our tithe and offering into fertile, productive soil. Often Christians find themselves giving repeatedly into "storehouses" that do little to advance the gospel or meet human need. Some even give to organizations that promote programs in clear opposition to biblical teaching. Just as it is possible to pray amiss, it is possible to give amiss.

In the Hebraic community of old, the tithe and offerings were deposited into a system directed by the priests and Levites that provided funding for the Temple, for the underprivileged in society, and for times of economic hardship or disaster. In the apostolic era, however, the priesthood of all believers was restored so that now all believers are responsible not only to give their tithe and offerings but also to discern to what need they should be given as they are directed by the Holy Spirit.

The tenth of increase has always been considered to be holy or separated unto the Lord (Leviticus 27:30). The Israelites were commanded to bring the firstfruits of their harvest (the tithe) to the Lord. When one had fully tithed and confessed his heritage, he was to attest that he had taken the tithes out of his house and had brought them to the priesthood, thereby fulfilling God's commandment.

Once he had made this affirmation, he was permitted to pray this petition for blessing: "Look down from heaven, your holy dwelling place, and bless your people Israel and the land you have given us" (Deuteronomy 26:15, NIV). The declaration of blessing was then placed upon the worshipper: "You have declared this day that the LORD is your God and you will walk in his ways.... The LORD had declared this day that you are his people, his treasured possession" (Deuteronomy 26:17-18, NIV).

Because the believer had brought his treasure to God, he was declared to be God's treasure! Then God promised, "And all these blessings shall come upon you and overtake you, because you obey the voice of the LORD your God: The LORD will command the blessing on you ... in all to which you set your hand. The LORD will open the heavens, the storehouse of his bounty" (Deuteronomy 28:2, 8, 12).

The language here is exactly what Malachi promises: the windows of heaven will be opened with uncontainable blessing to those who demonstrate their dependence and faithfulness to God through the act of tithing. Such obedience is foundational to receiving God's blessing, for God can never bless anything of which he does not approve. King David wisely described this divine law: "Delight yourself in the LORD, and he will give you the desires of your heart. Commit your way to the LORD; trust also in him, and he will do it" (Psalm 37:4-5, NIV).

The blessings of God are secure unto those who fulfill the instructions of his Word. Listen to this promise: "Now it shall be, if you diligently obey the LORD your God, being careful to do all his commandments ... All these blessings will come upon you and overtake you if you obey the LORD your God" (Deuteronomy 28:1-2, NASB). The blessings of God are inescapable for those who love God and demonstrate their love as Abraham did through his faithfulness to God's will and Word.

Tithing and giving, then, are the scriptural means of preparing a highway for a convoy of God's blessings. Those who are obedient to God's commandments in regard to money and other resources discover that they release God to bless all the works of their hands (Deuteronomy 16:15). Their generosity causes their entire human experience to be filled with the divine light. It is the key to the strongbox of God's treasure, and it is divine insurance that the richest of God's blessings will always belong to them.

CHAPTER 10

The One-Word Blessing

Is it possible to encapsulate all of God's blessings for humanity in one word? Can everything that God has planned be summed up a single word? If the apostle understood that all God is can be expressed in the word *love* (1 John 4:8), why would it not be possible to focus God's desires for humankind in one word also?

From the record of Scripture, it would appear to be so. There is one biblical word that has continually echoed God's blessing for man across the corridors of time. It is the Hebrew word *shalom*, which fundamentally means "peace," but also means much more than that. It means peace in the sense of the absence of conflict. It means peace that comes with health and security. It means peace that produces completeness, soundness, tranquility, and contentment. It means peace that guards quietness and prosperity. In short, it means everything that human beings need to be at peace.

Shalom is the final word in "The Blessing" that God dictated to Moses to be placed upon his children throughout their generations. "The LORD turn his face toward you and

The One-Word Blessing

שָׁלוֹם

Shalom

give you peace [*shalom*]" (Numbers 6:26). *Shalom* has always been and will always be God's final word for humankind. The blessing of the Lord brings peace, as David declared: "The LORD will bless his people with peace [*shalom*]" (Psalm 29:11).

Perhaps this is the reason that the word *shalom* has become both the greeting and the goodbye for the Jewish people for generations. One does not say, "Hello," or "Goodbye" in Israel. One simply says, "*Shalom!*" Could it be that the overriding concern among the Hebrew people for expressing blessing in every life situation came to be vocalized in this one word: "*Shalom*," the final word of God's blessing?

David recognized that the future of a man of integrity is *shalom* (Psalm 37:37). Solomon understood that God's commandments brought long life and *shalom* (Proverbs 3:1-2). Isaiah believed that God would keep the person who trusted in the Lord in perfect *shalom* (Isaiah 26:3). Jeremiah foresaw that after much trouble, God would restore *shalom* to his people (Jeremiah 33:6). Even the pagan kings Nebuchadnezzar and Darius addressed their subjects by saying, "*Shalom* be unto you" (Daniel 4:1; 6:25). Haggai's prophetic promise was, "In this place I will give *shalom* " (Haggai 2:9).

Isaiah predicted that a child would be born in Israel who would bear the title, "Prince of Peace," the "*Sar Shalom*" (Isaiah 9:6). He continued by declaring that of the increase of his *shalom* there would be no end (Isaiah 9:7). When the child that the prophet predicted was born, angels made this proclamation to Judean shepherds: "Glory to God in the highest, and on earth peace [*shalom*], goodwill to men" (Luke 2:14). As he walked among men, the Prince of Peace continually spoke this blessing: "*Shalom!*" He said it when he calmed the raging sea (Mark 4:39). He repeated it when he healed the sick (Luke 8:48). He spoke the calming word twice to his troubled disciples when he appeared to them after the resurrection (John 20:19, 21).

"Grace and peace be unto you" became Paul's familiar greeting in his letters to the churches (Romans 1:7; 1 Corinthians 1:3; Galatians 1:3; Ephesians 1:2). Peter, John, and Jude also used the same greeting. Each of the apostles continued in the rich Hebraic tradition that was foundational to their faith by speaking *shalom* into the lives of those to whom they ministered.

There is, then, a one-word blessing that speaks all of God's intentions for humanity. It is the word *shalom*. And there is a peace that passes all understanding (Philippians 4:7), the *shalom* of God that he has promised and will ever give to his children. In the time when the Messiah shall come, he will bring universal peace. The entire world then will hear the final word of God's blessing for man: *Shalom!*

O that all men everywhere would join in a mighty, resounding chorus that would echo unto the ends of the earth, speaking in unison God's one-word blessing: "*Shalom!*" Yes, may there be peace on earth speedily and in our lifetime!

CHAPTER 11

God's Final Blessing

It is safe to say that in everything God will have the last word. The first thing that God did in creation was to bless humanity, and the last thing that he will do when his kingdom finally comes is to bless them. In Eden, God blessed Adam and Eve by giving them dominion over all the earth. In the end, God will bless all the righteous with these words: "Come, you blessed of my Father, inherit the kingdom prepared for you from the foundation of the world" (Matthew 25:34). God's original blessing will be God's final blessing. What he promised humanity in the beginning will be restored fully in the end and with the amazing gift of eternal life that will even eclipse the blessing of paradise in the Garden of Eden!

God is ever a blessing God. With God, there was blessing in the beginning, there will be blessing in the end, and there is blessing everywhere in between. His mercies never come to an end. They are new every morning. Great is his faithfulness (Lamentations 3:22-23).

God's final Blessing

"Come, you blessed of my Father,
inherit the kingdom prepared for you
from the foundation of the world"
(Matthew 25:34).

Therefore, with David, we will "sing of the mercies of the LORD forever," making known his faithfulness to all generations (Psalm 89:1). With Paul we exclaim, "Blessed be the God and Father of our Lord Jesus Christ, who has blessed us with every spiritual blessing in heavenly places in Christ" (Ephesians 1:3). And with John and the holy angels and the millions of saints, we proclaim: "Blessing, and honor, and glory, and power, be to him that sits on the throne, and to the Lamb forever and ever" (Revelation 5:13).

A Personal Blessing

Of all the profound blessings that God has brought into my life, one of the greatest has been a comprehensive understanding of the biblically Hebraic foundations of the Christian faith. Understanding Christianity's Jewish roots has become a golden key that for me continually unlocks the treasures of Holy Scripture. The faith of Jesus and the apostles becomes vibrantly alive when it is placed in the context from which it emerged. God's covenant faithfulness is a rock of stability in which one can trust implicitly.

For over forty years I have been researching and writing, teaching and preaching foundational truths about how the original church of the first century developed from the matrix of God's covenant faith that was first established in Abraham. It has become more and more reassuring to understand that Jesus Christ is indeed the same yesterday, today, and forever and that the God of Scripture never changes.

No better example of God's unchanging hand could be offered than his consistent application of his eternal intentions for humanity. God determined to bless humankind in the beginning, and nothing could ever stop the fulfillment of his purposes. He has literally moved all of heaven and earth to ensure that his original blessing for the human race would be fulfilled in his final blessing.

Blessing, however, is but a single drop of water in an ocean of understanding about the Eternal God that awaits those who will diligently seek him by searching the Scriptures that testify of him (John 5:39). The mercies of God are limitless, new every morning (Lamentations 3:23). His truth endures to all generations despite all efforts to distort, pollute, and destroy what he has clearly declared (Psalm 100:5).

There is so much more to be studied, so much more to be learned. We have only begun to see a glimmer of the light that is too wonderful for human comprehension. Like Israel of old, we must learn to put the light upon a lampstand so that it will illuminate the entire house of God (Matthew 5:15). As we do, we will find that God will intensify the light even sevenfold (Isaiah 30:26) so that we gain insight and strength that will stabilize our lives and strengthen our salvation (Isaiah 33:6).

Now, we are sifting through the rubble of human tradition that has buried the bedrock of truth and the foundation stones of faith. We are working our way through layer after layer of accretions that accumulated during the centuries in which the church was Hellenized and Latinized and even paganized. It is easy to be distracted by the baubles of human tradition; however, we continue digging, determined to discover the jewels of truth that await us.

This is the primary purpose of Hebraic Christian Global Community (HCGC), the expanded networking organization that I founded more than twenty years ago. Thousands of people throughout the world who share a common burden for Hebraic restoration are coming together to share ideas and resources in the interest of impacting all of Christianity with this message of restoration.

Hebraic Christian Global Community is a nonprofit educational, publishing, and fellowship resource to the body of Christ. The vision of HCGC is to renew Christianity's Hebraic heritage by recovering the historical and theological foundations of the gospel of Jesus Christ, developing the concept and its practical applications, and encouraging its implementation in the church.

I am privileged to edit and publish *Restore!*, a cutting-edge journal that brings sound scholarship to bear on issues of vital importance to the church at large by featuring articles by international scholars from a wide range of denominational backgrounds. Through this vehicle, we have been able to enrich the lives of countless people with restoration truths and practices. I also edit and publish *Hebraic Insight*, an inductive Bible study journal for individuals, families, study groups, and congregations that helps believers who are searching for the Jewish roots of their faith to be established in the foundational Christian doctrines and practices that were manifest in the teachings of Jesus and the apostles. Additionally, I am constantly producing new books on various subjects of interest to believers who are serious about biblical discipleship.

Jesus well said it: "You shall know the truth, and the truth shall make you free" (John 8:32). The glorious liberty that insight into eternal truth brings is exhilarating, but it is also awesome. The challenge of Hebraic faith is to study so that we may do, thereby fulfilling God's instructions. When we become doers of the Word, we actually find that our doing God's Word becomes teaching. We find ourselves dynamically modeling God's truth, and we and others find that it works.

I trust that as you have read this volume you have received a greater passion for biblical truth and the blessing that it brings to the lives of those who discover it and make it a part of their lifestyle. You will now find yourself hungry to learn more about the Jewish roots of our Christian faith. Let me assure you that there is an inexhaustible storehouse awaiting you as you use your golden key to unlock the treasure chest of God's blessings.

May we together commit ourselves to the task of finding our way back home: back to the Bible; back to the experience of Jesus and the apostles; back to the richness of God's family tree of salvation and covenant experience, back to the faith once delivered to the saints. I stand ready to assist you in reclaiming the Hebraic foundations of your faith. Let me know how I can serve you.

May the LORD bless you and keep you. May the LORD cause his face to shine upon you and be gracious unto you. May the LORD turn his face toward you and give you peace. In the name of the Prince of Peace, Jesus Christ, our Lord. Amen.

Dr. John D. Garr
Pentecost, 2009

Meet the Author

Dr. John D. Garr is the founder and president of Hebraic Christian Global Community (formerly Restoration Foundation), an international, transdenominational, multi-ethnic networking organization—a coalition of scholars, church leaders, and laypersons who seek to restore the church to biblical Christianity by recovering and implementing the Hebraic foundations of the Christian faith.

Dr. Garr is also president and CEO of Hebraic Heritage Christian Center, an Atlanta-based institution of higher education that features a curriculum that is totally based on Christianity's Hebraic roots and is delivered by way of the Internet to students around the world.

Dr. Garr's teaching ministry is unique in that it combines excellent scholarship with intense spirituality and personal integrity. He is a theologian with extensive and diversified training. At the same time, he is a minister with a history of more than forty years of wide-ranging service to the international church. An academician with a pastor's heart, he is able to contextualize the great central truths of orthodox Christian faith in terms that laypersons can understand and incorporate into their lives. His ministry features teaching and preaching that challenges believers to faith that is manifest in a biblically sound, Christocentric lifestyle, grounded in the Hebraic heritage of Jesus and the apostles.

Dr. Garr's credentials include a Bachelors Degree in Theology, a Masters Degree in Theology (*summa cum laude*), a Doctor of Philosophy degree in Church Administration, and a Doctor of Theology degree from Evangelical Theological Seminary.

Having been called to Christian ministry at an early age, Dr. Garr has served the body of Christ in many ministerial capacities, including evangelist, pastor, overseer, presbyter, missionary, church planter, conference speaker, teacher, and seminary professor. In each of these capacities, he has served with integrity and distinction, applauded by both leaders and those whom he has served.

A prolific writer, Dr. Garr has authored many books, including most recently *Our Lost Legacy: Christianity's Hebrew Heritage; The Hem of His Garment: Touching the Power in God's Word; Living Emblems: Ancient Symbols of Faith; Christian Celebrations for Passover; God's Lamp, Man's Light: Mysteries of the Menorah; Bless You!: Restoring the Biblically Hebraic Blessing; Family Sanctuary: Restoring the Biblically Hebraic Home; Jesus: When God Became Human; Feminine & Free: God's Design for Women; The*

Church Dynamic: Hebraic Foundations for Christian Community; Christian Fruit: Jewish Root; Appointments with God. He is currently writing many other books to chronicle both historically and theologically the emergence of Christianity from the matrix of biblical Judaism, the subsequent Hellenization and Latinization of the church, the resultant Judaeophobia, anti-Judaism, and anti-Semitism that have characterized the church for nearly eighteen centuries, and the work of restoration that has been underway for the past five centuries to recover the church's biblical heritage.

He serves as editor and publisher of *Restore!*, the official journal of Hebraic Christian Global Community. He has contributed hundreds of essays and theological studies to various magazines and journals. He also writes, edits, and publishes *Hebraic Insight,* a Bible-study journal that encourages inductive Hebraic learning by individuals, families, study groups, and congregations. Another of his documentary series is called *Stability*, featuring volumes of studies in the foundational truths of Hebraic Christianity.

Another significant feature of this ministry is *New Treasures* media resources that provides continuing CD and DVD productions of Dr. Garr's lectures and sermons that help Christians reclaim the Jewish roots of their faith.

For many years, Dr. Garr has cultivated his calling to promote unity in the international body of Christ. He offers the unique ability to create dialogue on polarized issues in theology and polity and to bring forth the consensus of a common ground upon which all can stand. He has extensive training and experience in facilitating dialogue.

Through Hebraic Christian Global Community and other organizations, he promotes the biblical concept of unity in the pluriformity of diversity rather than the traditional concept of unity through uniformity and creedalism. Dr. Garr teaches that believers can be united in central theology while having latitude and flexibility in the areas of peripheral theology.

For twenty years, Hebraic Christian Global Community, the educational and publishing organization that is a resource to the entire body of Christ, has been the focus of Dr. Garr's ministry. HCGC was developed to meet the growing need in the international church for a forum that brings together scholars, church leaders, and laypersons for the purpose of analyzing the Jewish roots of Christian faith and to discover means of promoting and implementing the church's return to its biblical heritage. Dr. Garr believes that an over-Hellenized and over-Latinized church needs to recover its inherent Judaic ideals in order to be more Christian (in the sense of being more like Christ, her Jewish Lord) and in order to bring true maturity into the lives of believers.

Long an advocate of higher education that is focused in the Hebraic foundations of the Christian faith, Dr. Garr, in collaboration with scholars from around the world, has now launched Hebraic Heritage Christian Center. A completely new concept in academia, this college features a curriculum developed around the historical and theological truths of Christianity's Jewish roots. It is the answer to growing world-wide demand for superior quality education that focuses on biblical truths and avoids centuries of Hellenic and Latin tradition that has severed most of the church from its Jewish roots. The college is also unique in that all of its curriculum is delivered by means of the Internet in a revolutionary new learning system that the college has developed in order to ensure that its program is learner centered and learner friendly. Dr. Garr serves as chairman of the board, chancellor, and CEO for the college.

Dr. Garr has made numerous visits to Israel, where he has interacted with the Christian and Jewish communities, building bridges of dialogue and communication. He is currently working with rabbis in Jerusalem, encouraging them to bring their understanding of Judaism to Christians internationally so that the church can better understand Jews and Judaism and can seek ways in which they can cooperate in stemming the tide of neo-paganism, Platonism, and monism that is sweeping through western society.

In order to further his vision for educating the body of Christ as to its Hebrew foundations, Dr. Garr is collaborating with various scholars and church leaders in seminars and symposiums throughout the world. He has taught these concepts on five continents and in over twenty nations to pastors, leaders, and scholars of over fifty denominations. The teaching has been received with great acclaim because of the balanced biblicity that it features, its non-threatening style, and the absence of either legalism or antinomianism.

Dr. Garr has been married to the former Pat Hall (B.S. Business Administration, Covenant College) of Knoxville, Tennessee, for the past forty-five years. They have three sons, John David II (M.S. Mechanical Engineering, Tennessee

Technological University, M.S. Environmental Engineering, University of Alabama, engineer and flight controller for NASA's Johnson Space Center in Houston, Texas), Timothy Daniel (B.S. Chemical Engineering, Tennessee Technological University, engineer and production specialist for Dow Chemical Company in Houston, Texas), and Stephen Michael (Pharm.D., University of the Sciences at Philadelphia, pediatric pharmacist, Lubbock, Texas). They have three grandchildren, John David III, Lillian Faith, and Daniel Caleb. The Garrs reside in Atlanta, Georgia.

Understanding the Jewish roots of our faith is a golden key that unlocks the treasures of Holy Scripture and enriches Christian lives. This fundamental concept is the focus of Hebraic Christian Global Community, an international, transdenominational, multicultural publishing and educational resource for Christians.

Hebraic Christian Global Community features individuals and congregations who share the vision for restoring Christianity's Hebraic foundations, for networking together in true community, and for returning the church to a biblical relationship of loving support for the international Jewish community and the nation of Israel.

We publish *Restore!* magazine, a high-quality journal featuring theological balance and scholarly documentation that helps Christians recover their Hebrew heritage while strengthening their faith in Jesus.

We also publish *Hebraic Insight,* a quarterly Bible-study journal that assists individuals, families, study groups, and congregations in inductive Hebraic study of the Scriptures that is accurate, balanced, and trustworthy.

We distribute *Golden Key* books in order to disseminate high-quality teaching about Christianity's Hebraic foundations that is non-threatening and non-judgmental and helps believers follow the leading of the Holy Spirit in their lives.

We also provide various media resources through *New Treasures* media productions. Many of these can be accessed on our website.

The ministry of Hebraic Christian Global Community is made possible by our many partners around the world who share in our *Golden Key Partnership* program. We invite you to join us in sharing the satisfaction of knowing that you are a partner in an organization that is making a difference in the world by restoring Christians to their biblically Hebraic heritage, by eradicating Judaeophobia and anti-Semitism, by supporting Israel and the international Jewish community, and by encouraging collaborative efforts among those who share this vision.

For information about Hebraic Christian Global Community and all our resources and services, contact us at:

Hebraic Christian Global Community
P. O. Box 421218
Atlanta, GA 30342
www.HebraicCommunity.org

HEBRAIC HERITAGE

CHRISTIAN CENTER

Hebraic Heritage Christian Center is an institution of higher education that is dedicated to the vision of restoring a Hebraic model for Christian education. A consortium of scholars, spiritual leaders, and business persons, the Center features a continually developing curriculum in which each course of study is firmly anchored in the Hebrew foundations of the Christian faith.

The Hebraic Heritage Christian Center vision combines both the ancient and the most modern in an educational program that conveys knowledge, understanding, and wisdom to a worldwide student population. The Center seeks to restore the foundations of original Christianity in order to equip its students with historically accurate, theologically sound understanding of the biblical faith that Jesus and the apostles instituted and practiced. At the same time the Center endeavors to implement the finest in innovative, cutting-edge technology in a distance-learning program that delivers its user-friendly courses by the Internet.

Among the wide range of services and products that Hebraic Heritage Christian Center offers are the publications of Hebraic Heritage Press. These are delivered both in traditional print media as well as in electronic media to serve both the Center's student population and the general public with inspiring and challenging materials that have been developed by the Center's team of scholars.

Those who are interested in sharing in the development of Hebraic Heritage Christian Center and its commitment to restoring the Jewish roots of the Christian faith are invited to join the Founders' Club, people who support this team of scholars and leaders by becoming cofounders of this institution. Many opportunities for endowments are also available to those who wish to create a lasting memorial to the cause of Christian renewal and Christian-Jewish rapprochement.

Hebraic Heritage Christian Center
P. O. Box 450848
Atlanta, GA 31145
www.HebraicCenter.org

Other Books by Dr. Garr

God's Lamp Man's Light: Mysteries of the Menorah

The Hem of His Garment: The Power in God's Word

Bless You! The Power of the Biblical Blessing

Our Lost Legacy: Christianity's Hebrew Heritage

God and Women: Woman in God's Image and Likeness

Christian Celebrations for Passover

Jesus: When God Became Human

Church Dynamic: Foundations for Christian Community

Family Sanctuary: The Biblically Hebraic Home

Feminine by Design: God's Plan for Women

Touching the Hem: Jesus and the Prayer Shawl

www.HebraicCommunity.org

Get a Free Copy of

The Magazine That's Restoring the Biblically Hebraic Heritage to Christian Believers Around the World

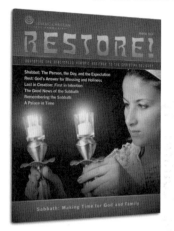

Restore! is the exciting journal that's:

✡ helping Christians recover the Jewish roots of their faith in Jesus Christ.

✡ fighting against Judaeophobia, anti-Judaism, and Antisemitism in the Christian church.

✡ encouraging Christians to support the international Jewish community and the nation of Israel.

✡ promoting the unity of cohesiveness in diversity within the body of Christ.

Here's what some of our readers are saying about *Restore!*

"*Restore!* is the best magazine I have ever read, the only one which I have read cover to cover." — Colyn King, Levin, New Zealand

"*Restore!* is an inspiration both in its quality and the profundity of its contents." — Jorge Robles Olarte, Medellin, Comumbia

"I consider *Restore!* to be the best magazine about Christianity's Jewish roots because of its quality, its scholarly articles, and most important, the strengthening of our faith." — Michael Katritsis, Athens, Greece

Discover for yourself the Jewish roots of your faith as you read the informative, provocative material in the pages of Restore!

❏ Please send me a free sample copy of *Restore!*
❏ Please enter my subscription to *Restore!* $35/yr. ($45/yr. outside US)
❏ Please bill my ❏ Visa ❏ AmEx ❏ Discover ❏ MasterCard

Card #_____ Exp_____ Security Code_____

Name_____ Phone _____

Address_____

City_____ State/Province____ Code_____ Nation____

Hebraic Christian Global Community
P.O. Box 421218, Atlanta, GA 30342 • 678.615.3568 • info@hebraiccommunity.org

Restore!

Hebraic Christian Global Community
P.O. Box 421218
Atlanta, GA 30342